NOT ALWAYS M

Ann ('Steve') He...
of Warrington a...
versity in Durh...
parish life until...
to work in the ...
interests include church and state, from
Mothers' Union to the City Magistrates' bench.
She has also been a contributor to 'Pause for
Thought' on BBC Radio 2's Derek Jameson
show.

STEVE ANN HENSHALL

Not always
MURDER
AT THE
VICARAGE

A view of
clergy marriage
today

Foreword by Eileen Carey

TRI△NGLE

First published 1991
Triangle
SPCK
Holy Trinity Church
Marylebone Road
London NW1 4DU

Second impression 1991

British Library Cataloguing in Publication Data

Henshall, Steve Ann E. *1933 –*
Not always murder at the vicarage: New look at
clergy.
1. Anglican Communion. Clergy. Households
I. Title
252.2

ISBN 0-281-04533-X

Typeset by Inforum Typesetting, Portsmouth
Printed in Great Britain by
BPCC Hazell Books
Aylesbury, Bucks, England
Member of BPCC Ltd.

Contents

Acknowledgements   ix

Foreword by Eileen Carey   xiii

1   CALLED TO SERVE GOD: *Clergy families as presented by the media today*   1

Past and present stereotypes — The media image — The savagery of the press — My own experience — Vicarage life — Moving to Liverpool Diocese and caring for clergy wives — Sources, materials, writing

2   YOU HAVE CALLED THESE YOUR SERVANTS: *Modern clergy and their backgrounds*   17

Clergy of today in a changed world — 'Lifetime' vocation — 'Late' vocation — Differing background and experience — Parochial expectations of new vicars and wives — Effect on families — Difficult decisions — Acceptance of change

3   OF GODLY LIFE AND SOUND LEARNING: *Training and the effect on families*   37

Families and churches facing up to change — Choices: non-residential course or college — Family life in

college — Housing problems —
Standard of living — Preparing for
parish life

4 SET THEM AMONG YOUR PEOPLE:
Living in the Vicarage   56

Lack of personal privacy — Blessed
Interruptions — Culture shock — Job
security and housing — Owning your
own home — Accommodation for
curates — Vicarage children

5 FELLOW SERVANTS IN CHRIST:
Parish, community and diocese   84

Working wives — Clergy husbands —
Choosing to stay at home — Clergy
couples in the community — Diocesan
attempts to affirm and support —
Mutual support — Spiritual
dimensions

6 NOT IN YOUR OWN STRENGTH:
When support is needed   109

Burnout — Counselling — Local
support — Stress factors — Marriage
breakdown — Broken Rites —
Bereavement — Retirement

7 POSTSCRIPT: *Bishops and their wives
are human too!*   134

Coping with change — Pubs, palaces
and prisons — Bishops' wives — House
or home: family isolation — New
bishops — The wider church —
Personal reflections

Appendix 1: 'Not Always Murder at the Vicarage'   153

Appendix 2: 'Parsons at Risk'   163

Further Reading   168

Acknowledgements

The information in this book is based largely on the experience of clergy couples in the Church of England. However, many of the situations described and the views expressed are shared equally by clergy of other Christian denominations.

Although names have been changed to protect their identity, these people are real. I am very grateful to all who have helped me by telling their stories. In addition to my own family, I particularly wish to thank the Archdeacon of Liverpool, Graeme Spiers, and his wife Ann, and the Liverpool Diocesan Director of Ordinands, Bob Metcalf, and his wife Rachel, all wise in their understanding of the advantages and disadvantages of vicarage life today.

Steve Ann Henshall
December 1990

For
clergy couples everywhere
and especially those
in the
Diocese of Liverpool

Foreword

It gives me great pleasure to write this Foreword to Steve's book because it is a subject close to my heart. For nearly thirty years now I have been involved in my husband's ministry as wife of an ordinand, curate, vicar, theological college tutor, then principal, diocesan bishop – and now wife of the Archbishop of Canterbury! So I can identify with much of what she is saying.

Regrettably, much of the publicity given to this subject has been negative in the past and the impression is given that all is 'doom and gloom' in the vicarage. Many of us, however, know that is a one-sided perspective because we have personal experience of the joys and privileges and immense job satisfaction to be found in vicarage life.

Steve has not written about this very controversial subject lightly but rather because she has spent many years as wife and mother in a vicarage and has become disenchanted with media coverage of the issue. Why is it, we may ask, that the experience of the vicar's wife receives such interest – it is hardly the fate of the wife of a doctor or lawyer, for example! Yet the TV, radio and papers seem to portray the vicarage family in a negative vein.

From my experience I would like to focus particularly on three areas of importance.

First, attention is drawn in chapter three to theological colleges. Having been closely involved in the life of three such institutions I am able better than most to see the opportunities as well as the deficiencies of present patterns of training. The involvement of wives in the life of colleges sets forward models which, for better or worse, are taken on into parish life. For example, a college may give the most excellent theological training, making major demands on the ordinand's time, failing to see that the pressure placed on the wife to bear the financial burden of the home as well as the emotional stress of the move and care of children may all be contributing causes to later problems in ministry. On the other hand, there is the testimony of so many wives that there in the college setting they found their own vocation to be a clergy wife, or to recognise the importance of their own calling as a mother or as a professional in another sphere – a nurse, teacher, social worker or whatever. It is indeed possible that the new reality of clergy husbands may call on the church to look afresh at some of these issues. I believe that Steve has pointed the way forward in a number of such areas.

Another point of significance in the book is that of family life discussed in chapter four. As I read it I could not help but think of our experience. We had the great fortune of going as curate and wife to a wonderful vicar and Mrs Vicar who – they would be too modest to say this – modelled a happy and fulfilled Christian marriage. Our relationship with them was formative, rich and deep. This was in spite of the fairly depressing physical circumstances in which we lived – an old, damp cottage with a small backyard. There were times when we complained about the place we lived in, and it has to be said that the material conditions of ministry today are far, far better. But at times like that we recalled that our lot was no worse – indeed, a lot better – than many who lived in the huge flats that rose all around us. At least we had a backyard – even if it was made up of tombstones! Yes, we were hard-up, cripplingly at times, but the help given by the congregation we served was often unbelievably generous. It was a tough apprenticeship but altogether a positive experience that prepared us for what lay ahead. Our seven years in a vicarage in the north of England was very different but equally fulfilling. We lived in a seven-bedroomed vicarage which we found impossible to heat adequately. Against that we had the space we needed for four healthy and active youngsters and for my widowed mother who needed care and attention. We had a wonderfully supportive congregation there also who assisted, and the size of the house had the advantage of giving us plenty of room for visitors.

Both these experiences had their negative as well as positive sides but the latter clearly outweighed the former – and it is the positive we all now recall. Steve brings the experience of many people into this chapter and we are shown the honest, candid and revealing experiences of people who have lived in vicarages.

This Foreword would not be complete if I did not comment on chapter seven: 'Bishops and their wives are human too!' Yes, we are; and for most of us, becoming a bishop and a bishop's wife is the last thing we expected to happen to us. It is a strange, different life and there have been times, especially in our first year, when I felt isolated and cut off from other clergy wives. Add that to the fact that the bishop is expected to live in a grander house or palace and you can quickly lose that feeling of belonging that comes from being part of a parish or college. Yet there is no chance of the bishop's life ever becoming boring because of the sheer pressure of the job and the varied demands on those in this office. It is so easy to be tempted into thinking that the bishop is more important than others in Christian ministry. But we are not; the difference is simply that our terms of servanthood are different – our task is to serve the saints. So from the present reality of this episcopal ministry I was personally delighted by Steve's analysis of this subject. I have not seen anything written at any depth before on the situation of the bishop's wife and found her examination most helpful.

I am therefore delighted that Steve has decided to 'stand up and be counted' because her book gives us many valuable insights into the subject of vicarage life and, as many of us believe, it is worthy of wide circulation. Incidentally, her own humanity comes shining through, making the point that it is absolutely essential for those in ministry to have a sense of humour to survive.

Eileen Carey
Lambeth Palace

1
Called to Serve God

A vicar moved to a new parish. His son started at the local secondary school and soon made friends. In time he went to their homes. However, he never suggested that any of them should come back to his house after school. One day, some of them started to walk along with him. They reached the rather pleasant detached house, standing in its spacious garden. They all stopped.

'Is this where you live then?' asked the other lads.

'Well,' came the rather unwilling reply, 'my mum cooks here.'

True or not, that story brings a conspiratorial smile of recognition to the faces of most vicarage families when they hear it!

Yet some of the most famous names in our country's history (and some of the most notorious) were clergy children. Great leaders like Lord Nelson, the poet Tennyson and the Brontë sisters, with their vivid imaginations, are among these. More recently, Field Marshal Montgomery and Laurence Olivier stand out, together with many well-known public figures of today in all walks of life, like the actor John Hurt, Virginia Wade the

1

tennis star, and the unabashed nude model, Fiona Richmond, to name but three who grew up in vicarages. It would be interesting to know whether their careers blossomed because they were happy as clergy children or because they reacted strongly against their upbringing. John Gummer, probably the best-known 'clergy son' MP, has said publicly that his present high church affiliation can be traced back to his own revolt against an evangelical father.

Past and present stereotypes

There has always been a tendency for parishioners to put their parsons on a pedestal: to want to believe that they are not subject to normal temptations. In the past this was easier to do because clergy and their families were more remote, usually well-educated and protected by servants. Their upper-class image was regarded with respect even if not with affection and they gave a sense of security and solid foundations. It is easy to portray them as worldly manipulators, as Trollope did so skilfully and cynically in novels like *Barchester Towers*, but the Victorian image still survives fairly intact in the national memory.

The modern vicar and his wife, while still suffering to a certain extent from these old expectations, have come to be seen very differently. The old stereotype has been replaced by one which seems to be even more misleading and unhelpful: the vicarage family under stress, with rebellious children, desperately seeking privacy while feeling that they live in a goldfish bowl.

2

The media image

In recent years, vicarage life seems to have had a particularly bad press. Parsons are always good for a laugh but sometimes this naïve image becomes tedious. Newspapers rarely mention them unless there is at least a whiff of scandal. Alan Bennett's tragi-comic Susan, the vicar's wife in 'Bed among the Lentils' (one of the portraits in his series *Talking Heads*), while brilliantly portraying certain aspects of the life, probably sums up the cynical view of many people outside the church ... perhaps some within it too? More serious than any of these however, is the fact that even documentary-type programmes like *Everyman* on BBC television and *Encounters* on ITV can be devoted to the subject. The clergy family has become a 'social problem', according to the media.

My own most recent involvement began in the winter of 1987. It was eleven years after I had left vicarage life myself when my husband, Michael, had become Bishop of Warrington and we went to work in the Liverpool diocese beside David Sheppard and his wife Grace. One Sunday morning, we visited one of our clergy who was dying of cancer. He was forty-two, the father of four children. We joined in the Eucharist together round a coffee table with him, his wife and their young son. Later that day we watched a programme in Central TV's *Encounter* series called 'Great Expectations' which was about clergy marriages. We could not help comparing what we both felt to be a very negative approach to the subject as it was presented by Michelle Guinness, to the wonderful support of the parishioners for the family in the vicarage where we had just spent the morning.

In my frustration, although agreeing with much that was said in the prográmme, I wrote to the producer, John Oxley, suggesting that there could have been a more positive approach, mentioning the supportive and community aspects of parish life. In his reply he said 'A considerable quantity of very valuable material had to be left on the cutting-room floor.'

At about the same time, an article I had written and had used with several groups of wives as a basis for discussion, was published in the *Church Times* under the title 'Not Always Murder at the Vicarage' (27 February 1987). (This is reproduced in Appendix 1.) This was an attempt to give a reasonably balanced view, showing some of the more pleasant aspects of the life and pointing out some of the distinct advantages when compared with lay families. I was overwhelmed by the response to my article. Clergy wives of all denominations wrote to me. Only one of the many letters I received suggested that I was telling clergy wives how lucky they were because I was looking back to my own vicarage days through rose-coloured spectacles. Many, including two other bishops' wives, asked when I was going to write a book on the subject.

Michelle Guinness wrote to the *Church Times* two weeks later. Her letter was very fair and clear, taking up some of the points I had made. It contains this admission which could have made such a difference to the ITV programme: 'Many of the couples I interviewed over eighteen months readily admitted the advantages of job security, belonging to a caring community, etc.' What a pity that part had to be left on the cutting-room floor! I absolutely agree with the rest of what Mrs Guinness said, including 'That does not alter the fact that most clergy wives struggle at times with the role and the expectations imposed on them — some to the point where they feel they can no longer cope.' I have discovered that the video of this programme is often shown to couples in training at theological colleges. I hope that other views are also promoted.

Since then there have been various other attempts by the media to dissect the problems of vicarage life, including one on *Woman's Hour* in July 1987, in an equally negative vein. In reply to my queries, the producer, Lyn Brookes, herself a clergy wife, wrote to me that articles like mine were often published in church newspapers. This was a fairly astounding assumption. The editor of the *Church Times* (then Mr Bernard Palmer) told me that it was quite incorrect, as almost everything he received on the subject tended to concentrate on difficult aspects.

The BBC *Everyman* series included Lyn in a programme about clergy wives on 14 February 1988. Among varied reactions to this particular attempt it seemed to be felt that the programme was generally not very representative. Many wives in our own diocese remarked that it was significant that no wife from an inner-city parish appeared on the programme, in spite of the fact that plenty cope with such areas and actually choose to bring up families there!

The savagery of the press

Apart from the obvious exaggerations of the gutter press when reporting anything remotely scandalous about clergy, especially if it has to do with sex, my own experience of manning the phone at such times has highlighted their ruthless approach. I have vivid memories of arriving with Michael at a church where the vicar had been having an affair with a parishioner. He and his wife (who stayed with him) were barricaded up in the vicarage, while about twelve reporters and cameramen descended on us like vultures. On other occasions as a result of press reports I have heard parochial clergy and bishops torn to shreds, deliberately in front of me, in school staffrooms and even once or twice by fellow magistrates. The critical and unkind attitude of the press towards the previous Archbishop of Canterbury and his wife shocked many bishops from abroad when visiting this country. The prevailing atmosphere of criticism and low expectations coupled with modern irreverence for all public figures, particularly politicians, extends equally to the clergy.

I can't believe that all this adverse publicity helps anybody. The public may find it hard to understand what vicarage life is really like, so will hardly be helped by a distorted and possibly unrealistic view. Equally, I believe that it can have only a bad effect on the families themselves. If ordinands and their families read pessimistic articles in newspapers or watch negative programmes on TV they will feel threatened before they even arrive in a parish. The parishioners will become 'them', some indefinable enemy, rather than fellow Christians with whom the clergy family hope to live in community. It can't be very encouraging to those who may be wondering if they might have a vocation to the ministry. Families already well entrenched in vicarage life may start to question whether they are happy after all. The worst result would seem to be when couples who probably would not have been happy whatever or wherever they were, start to blame their own problems on the job.

My own experience

When Michael and I got married, five weeks before he was ordained deacon, nobody suggested that there was anything particularly strange about the life we were about to embark on. No doubt some of my friends with traditional views smiled at the idea of me being a curate's wife, since I enjoyed nice clothes, wearing high heels, dancing and the theatre. I believed, as I still do, that these were all part of God's creation. I was amused when the girls in the youth club told me they had been surprised (and pleased) to see that I was not at all like they expected as I had curly hair and wore makeup! I have never thought of Christianity as dull: hard, certainly, but not a long-faced religion.

The standard picture of a clergy wife in 1956 was of a faceless figure in tweeds and brogues, with her hair pulled back in a bun, wearing a frightful hat. In spite of the fact that the domestic and economic changes brought about during two world wars had radically altered the conditions of life in the vicarage, just as everywhere else, marrying a clergyman was still considered highly respectable, rather boring and somewhat removed from normal life. Clergy marriages rarely came apart. If they did it was a cause of hushed scandal. Most parishioners appeared to take it for granted that the clergy household must find it easier than others to have a happy family life. Fortunately, there were always some who were more discerning and realized that the vicar and his family (if he had one) were human beings.

My own family's reactions at the time of my marriage were fairly typical of those of the world at large. My brothers assumed that I should always be poor (and was therefore to be pitied). They also imagined that we would spend the rest of our lives in some sort of ivory tower, far away from the cares of the real world. The reply from my father to my letter mentioning that we hoped to get married was rather dismissive. He suggested that my education had been wasted since I was going to be a vicar's wife. On the whole I think my family wrote me off, deciding that I must have religious mania.

Nobody seemed to think it necessary to explain to me what a 'difficult' time I was going to have. I was not prepared in any way for the 'expectations' of a parish. The 'problems' my children would have were not even hinted at! If that sounds sarcastic, it is really not intended that way. I know that nowadays theological colleges take infinite care to help husbands and wives and their families to prepare for parish life. This is very helpful and worthwhile. Today, over 50% of ordinands are married by the time they are accepted to train for the ministry, which is almost a complete reversal of the situation when I got married. Then, in some dioceses, clergy were not allowed to marry until they had served their first assistant curacy.

It seems to be a strange paradox that at a time when so much more care is given to preparation for vicarage life, there appears to be more general unhappiness in clergy families, not less, as might have been hoped and expected.

Vicarage life

At this point I must be completely honest in stating my own position and explain another reason which led me to write this book. I loved living in a vicarage – most of the time.

No doubt a psychiatrist would decide that in my case this was because it gave me security. My childhood was not very happy. I was sent away to school when I was ten and my parents finally parted when I was a student. I know it's true that I tried very hard to bring up my own family with a real sense of belonging, showing care for their own individual worth. I found the sense of community in the parishes where we lived a great source of strength and support. This is what I missed most when Michael became a bishop.

The first twenty years of our married life were spent in three parishes. We had three very happy years in Bridlington, while Michael was a curate in the York diocese. I was then a 'working wife' (a subject which will be touched on later in this book). Then we moved to the Chester diocese, where my husband had grown up. Our parish was not in the 'plush pastures' such as I had seen when I stayed there with his family! It was a mill town on the very edge of Cheshire, an ugly product of the Industrial Revolution called Mossley, though our part of the town was blessed with the pretty name of Micklehurst.

I had never seen anywhere quite like it in my life. Forgive me if that sounds condescending. In actual fact it is far from that in intention because I can honestly say that I have never met such wonderful people. I know, in retrospect, that I learned much more in our four years there than I ever did in my four years at university. There I saw 'real' life, great determination and hard work. Most of all, I understood the meaning of the extended family, both in the actual families themselves and in the wider community. They understood much more than I did about poverty and survival and they managed it all with a remarkable sense of humour.

After that, we suffered the heartbreak of pulling up our roots and moving once again, this time to a very different kind of parish in Altrincham, then a pleasant market town with a real sense of identity. The next twelve years were generally very happy, as we worked hard to establish a 'community' rather than just a 'congregation' at the parish church, which had become very run-down and inward-looking. We lived with our three children in a pleasant, manageable vicarage. There were moments in those years when I would have liked to bar the door and cut the telephone wires. I read the 'fed-up' moans of other graduate housewives in the women's page of the *Guardian* with sisterly feeling. But on the whole at that time I was too busy and occupied to ask myself whether I liked being a clergy wife or not.

Then one morning in November 1973, I was reading the *Church Times* when an article by Michael Smout (some of which is reproduced in Appendix 2) made me hop round the kitchen in dismay and a certain amount of disbelief. The title was 'Parsons at Risk'. While I agreed with much of what he wrote, I was taken aback by his main point that the clergy are 'more than usually prone to matrimonial and other problems'.

I was surprised. I knew the clergy in the area where we lived fairly well, and while none appeared to have perfect marriages most had good partnerships. It seemed to me that there were no more and no fewer unhappy marriages among them than among the couples I knew in secular jobs. I come from a legal family myself, and there is plenty of unhappiness and boredom in that profession.

While I was still ruminating on this article, I discovered that the local clergy, meeting together in our parish that week, were also rather put out by it and did not agree with its main thesis. I wrote a letter to a newspaper — for the first time in my life — and it appeared in the *Church Times* on 7 December 1973 (quoted in full in Appendix 2). In it are the 'germs' of my later article and ultimately of this book. That was the beginning of my interest and involvement in the whole subject of vicarage life on a wider scale than the somewhat limited experience of my own life up till then.

I was made to think even more about how other wives saw it from the two letters which followed my own. One was from a very unhappy 'clergy wife' of two years' standing, who had been married eleven years. She and her husband were planning to part six months later when he would be due to move. She wrote: 'I think the risk for mature-student ordinands is far greater because their wives have had a previous existence, where their husband was truly a husband and father. How does one accept (without nagging) the idea of being a part-time wife?' This letter was followed by one from Bob Wilkes, then an ordinand at an Anglican theological college, and chairman of the Anglican Ordinands Committee. He wrote:

> Too many students while at college have expressed intense personal tensions in their marriages, financial affairs and so on . . . Too often the wives of students are only superficially involved in the training which absorbs their husbands' time and energy. The result is that they are not prepared for the life as the wife of a parson, often with their own job to do as well.

Both these letters opened my eyes to problems which I had not encountered personally. I never saw vicarage life in quite the same way after that!

Moving to Liverpool diocese: caring for clergy wives

The biggest change in the life of our family came in 1976, when we moved to Liverpool diocese. This meant taking children of fifteen, thirteen and eleven out of a parish into a completely different environment. We lost our close, local community with its inbuilt support systems, including babysitters! Our predictable pattern of family meals and time off together also suffered a severe blow. If you are used to living in a vicarage, it is surprising how much you realize what you have taken for granted when this is no longer the case. Our children found it an unsettling experience and I personally felt quite 'bereaved' for a time.

As I gradually got to know more clergy wives in the Liverpool diocese, I began to understand how varied their lives were. Each parish, each vicarage, each family is unique. Through the years since then, I have visited many of their homes and appreciate increasingly what an interesting, dedicated and loving group of women they are.

At a diocesan evening for clergy wives some years ago, our speaker was Mrs Ann Booth-Clibborn, wife of the Bishop of Manchester. After her talk, which was realistic, amusing and down to earth, she asked everybody to write down three things. These were: what was BEST about being a clergy wife, what was WORST and lastly, what could be done about the second. I took these replies home to make some kind of evaluation to help our preparations for the next diocesan clergy wives' conference. There were about sixty altogether, all anonymous. The most interesting fact was that the same answer was given by almost equal numbers to both the best and worst things. It was 'living in the vicarage'. The saddest reply of all read: 'The BEST thing: Nothing. The WORST thing: Being a clergy wife. What I can do about it: Have as many friends as possible outside the church.' I wished I knew who she was. At least she had been brave enough, or lonely enough, to come.

This contrasted sharply with my own feelings when I lived in a vicarage myself and it nagged at the back of my mind. At about the same time, I read a book to which a number of clergy wives had contributed, called *Married to the Church*. As a result of these experiences and those already mentioned earlier in this chapter, I have finally been encouraged to find out for myself how clergy families really do feel today.

Sources, material and writing

It would be quite unprofessional — and impossible — to attempt to write simply from my own experience. So I have talked or written to a great number of clergy families, especially wives and children, in eleven dioceses in addition to my own. I have been in touch with ordinands' wives during their husbands' training and afterwards when they have experienced the reality of parish life for themselves. In visits to theological colleges, I have met men and women in training and their families and also listened to members of staff. I have also heard from parishioners about how they view vicarage life. These include friends and relations of clergy, some of whom, while appreciating the loss of privacy, have expressed some envy about the job security and freedom from anxiety about housing and mortgages which they feel are often undervalued by the clergy.

Many also mentioned the job satisfaction so often resulting from a sense of vocation.

It has been a fascinating experience in every way. I have learned a great deal, particularly about the background of modern ordinands, their present training and the conditions which families often endure during that period. I have been slightly astonished and very privileged by the frankness and honesty with which so many people have spoken to me. The greatest shock has been to discover the true extent of marriage breakdown among clergy families. Michael Smout may have been ahead of his time in 1973 but I believe that for a variety of reasons he could use his title 'Parsons at Risk' again today with a whole new agenda. This would include the increase in the numbers of working wives, late vocations and expectations of support.

My own family has contributed comments of every hue! My father-in-law was ordained shortly after my husband. He used to speak from his own experience of the trauma of late vocation. At the time of writing, one of our two sons is a single curate in a depressed area in the North East. My daughter is a curate's wife (after swearing in the past that she would never marry a clergyman). She started married life nine storeys high in a tower block in Merseyside. None of us has reached our present situations without many difficulties and questions along the way. There have been plenty of times when we might well have wept — and sometimes did — but fortunately we all possess a sense of humour, particularly about ourselves.

Most of all though, without sounding too pious about it, I believe that what makes it possible is the undergirding belief that this is God's work in the world. However hard it may be to remember at times — when there's an emergency, when the third meal is interrupted in a day — we know, really, that it is a privilege.

I realize that by writing this book, I shall be exposing myself to being condemned as what Michelle Guinness called the 'proverbial ostrich', but I have decided to stand up and be counted because I still believe there is plenty to say that is positive about our life. Other voices, those who do not find that it is all bad, should be heard on the subject of life in the vicarage. I know many very happy, fulfilled vicars' wives and plenty of clergy children who are no more disturbed or deprived than any of their peers. Of course, I also know and care for many unhappy clergy couples, families who are not coping, single clergy and women deacons who often find life very lonely. My contention is that these are usually the only people we seem to hear about in the media. I have discovered that my own frustration at this one-sided view is shared by many others. There are plenty of funny books written about clergy life but this is not one of them, although I hope there is room for amusement in its pages. It will never be possible to sum up in any comprehensive way what is surely one of the most interesting, fulfilling, infuriating, yet still one of the most worthwhile 'jobs' in the world.

2
You Have Called These Your Servants

*MODERN CLERGY AND THEIR
BACKGROUNDS*

During the twentieth century people's attitudes towards the clergy have changed dramatically. When my mother was a little girl, before the first world war, she and her twin sister always viewed Canon Nolloth of Beverley Minster with considerable fear. He remained in her memory as an awesome figure, highly respected and respectable, who drove around in a pony and trap. His lady wife sat beside him, wearing severe black clothes and a large hat. There was an aura of 'noblesse oblige' which obviously communicated itself to small children.

A generation later, my husband was a boy in Wilmslow, Cheshire. He recalls Rector Edwards, the epitome of the perfect gentleman, a Cambridge man, always wearing a pristine white tie. Until his death in office in the early 1940s, this distinguished, aristocratic amateur ran the parish from his very large, rather remote rectory. Parishioners tended to think that his stately wife modelled herself on Queen Mary (she of the toque . . .). Apart from the servants in the house there was also a driver, a flunky called Grice.

Others who remember the Edwards household speak of 'no suggestion of snobbery' but it is clear that however conscientious the rector was about his parochial duties, he also led a very active social life. Garden parties on the rectory lawn were big events, attended by smartly dressed families. When the next rector, Canon Reeman, arrived wearing a raincoat, Wilmslow society wondered whatever had hit them! In fact, he was to prove a much more active and involved parson, personally better equipped to understand his parishioners. Perhaps he was the shape of things to come.

Even today in Lancashire towns the attitude of respect for the parson persists. Many people remember how, in the depression of the 1930s, it was the clergy who organized the soup kitchens and arranged for needy families to be given warm clothes. Only a few years ago the present Rector of Wigan was stopped in the market place by an old man who asked him to shake hands with his grandson. He did so. 'Well now,' said the old man, his face beaming with gratitude, 'when you're old you'll be able to say that you once shook hands with the Rector of Wigan!'

Clergy of today in a changed world

Most modern parsons and their wives are a whole world away from these examples. There can be few professions where perceptions, conditions and public response have changed so much during this century, particularly in the last twenty years, both for better and for worse. Yet even those within the church itself often seem not to recognize this. I discovered great ignorance among some parishioners about their clergy, their training and their role. I also found that most do not appear to realize how many of the present generation are older, having a late vocation, often involving considerable upheaval in the lives of their families, sometimes with severe financial sacrifices. Such clergy and their wives, for their part, may find the expectations of a parish restricting or intrusive after the relative privacy of their previous experience. Curates who have held down highly responsible jobs in the past have told me how they found themselves treated in a condescending manner as new boys when they arrived in a parish as deacons. This can weigh particularly on wives, and on husbands of women deacons, some of whom see the change as their partner's vocation and have no wish to share in the practical details of it. Many of them will be in full-time work. It must be clear from these facts that some of the ingredients which cause the problems so attractive to the press, are already present.

The Church of England has never required that its clergy wives should be officially 'approved', unlike the Salvation Army, which insists that all wives should be fellow-officers with their husbands. I have heard it said, though, (by a bishop's wife!) that married candidates should take their partners to the selection conference with them when they first put themselves forward for training. These are organized by the Advisory Council for the Church's Ministry (ACCM). Many couples told me that they would have liked this but the questions which would arise from such an arrangement are many and varied and well beyond the scope of this book. However, forty years ago most clergy wishing to marry would be expected to obtain permission from the bishop. There are still couples who remember the ordeal of the episcopal interview. Jim, a bustling middle-aged vicar, laughed as he recounted how, as a highly nervous curate, he was in such a state that his collar stud came undone and he spent the whole time in a condition of near apoplexy. Engaged couples are still sometimes invited to meet the bishop together but nobody would expect him to be other than utterly charming and usually delighted to officiate at their wedding.

Our clergy come from the laity. In the past there was always a large group of upper- and middle-class men, with clear expectations of their future role in the community. At the beginning of this century, the place of the church was accepted, understood and largely unquestioned. Social change, brought about largely through the introduction of the welfare state, has removed much of the political and cultural significance of the church so that today it is seen by many, who only have a slight or nonexistent connection with it, as irrelevant, an anachronism from the past. Rabbi Jonathan Sachs, in the first of his Reith Lectures in 1990 on 'The Persistence of Faith', spoke of 'an emptiness at the heart of our common life. Something has been lost in our consumer culture: that sense of meaning beyond ourselves that was expressed in our great religious traditions.'

This situation has altered the context in which the clergy now exercise their ministry. It brings a sense of bewilderment and frustration to many, making them feel marginalized in a world where people are more likely to go for help to their doctor or a psychiatrist than to them.

'Lifetime' vocation

Michael and I first met on the university stage when we were students. He was passionately interested in the theatre. However, he had a strong sense of vocation from an early age, having been involved from childhood in his local parish and growing up in a very committed family. In those rather narrow-minded days, it was quite a problem at times to explain to friends that you could have interests that did not necessarily conflict with your Christian calling. Television was becoming very popular and there was just the hint of a temptation when it was suggested that he might make a career as a producer. Equally, a little earlier, Michael had very much enjoyed his National Service Life as an army officer in Germany after the war. Yet there was never any real defection from that inner certainty that he was called by God to be a priest.

I never knew him as anything other than an ordinand, so I have always felt that I should only have myself to blame if I turned round later and said I had not wanted to be a clergy wife. Yet I know that if anybody had told me, when I left school, that I should be married to a curate, I should have been very surprised! I was a practising Christian, not easy even in those days, with plenty of theological and liturgical knowledge gleaned from my school, St Hilda's at Whitby, but little practical experience of everyday parish life. I fancied a career in publishing or some related profession. In 1956 marriage would have made an independent career of that nature difficult to pursue, so as I loved Michael I decided to teach and stayed on for a year to do a postgraduate diploma in Education. We set out with starry-eyed visions of a life of relative poverty, a dilapidated vicarage with a large family, feeding all and sundry round the kitchen table and living happily ever after. It was not quite like that.

'Late' vocation

It is often a very different story from ours. Many men and women nowadays arrive at a stage, later in their lives, where they feel a strong sense that God is calling them to the ordained ministry. They may already be well established on a satisfying career, as a teacher, a chemist or a shop assistant, with a family and (not least!) a mortgage. In some cases it takes years to come to terms with the demands which become obvious and which if responded to, will in most cases affect not only themselves, since families may find great difficulty in accepting any suggestion of change.

There are all kinds of sparks which begin to glow until finally they flame up as the thought that will not go away. Rick had been a social worker. He said: 'Although I'd felt I had a call twenty years ago, I read John Robinson's *Honest to God* and got all mixed up . . . then I couldn't see how I could justify myself as a parish priest . . . I couldn't explain what he did.' It had taken all that time for him to let his glow become a fire. Henry had been moved by going into the silence of retreat for the first time. 'I had to listen for a change . . . by the end I realized that it was time I said YES to God.' Sudden conversions make some people feel that their next move must be ordination. This is generally discouraged for a time but may eventually prove to be right.

I asked Jane, a vicar's wife now in her forties, whose husband had a late vocation, how she had reacted when he had first confided in her with a very tentative 'I think I'd like to try to be a priest.' She said 'It was ten years ago. I said he should go ahead and try. I was happy for him.' She soon began to realize that they 'were going to have to leave a lot behind'. It was only after the first year had been completed that she felt she was beginning to understand what it really meant for her and their family.

Jenny, still in her twenties, first met her husband when he was an accountant. She said: 'I knew before our relationship developed into a committed one that Jim would be going to theological college. He went out to Japan for a year to work for Missions to Seamen while he was sorting it all out. I was very happy that he had discovered his true vocation and felt confident that he would feel fulfilled in it.' She is a vet. They married while he was training and she was able to continue with her own work.

Many wives who told me about their initial

response to their husbands' call saw it as a new opportunity for themselves as well. June and her husband had been married eleven years when he was ordained. He had been a self-employed musician and she worked full-time in middle management. She decided to give up her job to 'become a clergy wife and mother' (to their two young boys of five and three). She said: 'I knew before he did that he'd end up being ordained!'

Differing background and experience

Today's ordinands come from every conceivable kind of background, bringing skills and experience which are increasingly useful in communicating with parishioners. A theological college lecturer suggested to me that colleges sometimes ignore these gifts instead of affirming them for use in future ministry. Some people have quite chequered careers before they eventually become aware that God may be calling them to the ordained ministry.

Dick and Shirley live in a pleasant vicarage in the middle of a very poor, populous housing estate. Now in their forties, they say that they would never have believed it if a fortune teller had told them twenty years ago where they would be now. They married young when Dick was an instructor in the army. He had been a regular churchgoer until he was fifteen . . . 'boat-boy, crucifer, that sort of thing'. It all seemed 'rather soft' for a soldier so he stopped bothering. Shirley was only nineteen when their first baby was born. Dick came in one day and told her that he had made arrangements with the chaplain for the christening. 'He's going to do you at the same time', he told Shirley. She made no objection though she had no real church background. She said that it meant nothing at the time.

After sixteen years in the army Dick bought himself out. By now they had two children and for a time were dependent on their parents, living in the Midlands. Dick became an insurance salesman. He said: 'It taught me a lot about knocking on doors.' They went through a troubled period, insecure and unsure about where their future lay. Both remember the terrible day when Shirley opened the door to him, having steeled herself to break the news that she was pregnant again. He was equally fraught as he had just thrown up his job, so they were going to be dependent on her earnings as a secretary. He decided to go to college to get some qualifications since all his had been acquired in the army.

Meanwhile they had begun to go to church. When Dick, perhaps prompted by residual memories from his upbringing, went to the local curate to ask about his older children being confirmed, the reply had been, 'Fine. Bring them to church next Sunday.' They found themselves in the middle of an 'Evangelism Explosion' and became totally committed Christians.

Three years later, when Dick told Shirley he was convinced that God was telling him 'I want you in the ministry', she thought it was terrible and was adamant that he was not called. However, after a period which they both described as one of 'desperate unhappiness', during which Shirley became as convinced as he was that he really must respond to his true vocation, he was finally able to embark on theological training.

Dick and Shirley have never looked back since then. The gifts which both had found so useful in their secular jobs and their experiences of unemployment and insecurity in the past make them particularly understanding about the circumstances of many of their parishioners. They have been there themselves. Not least, they have been among the 'unchurched' and know how it feels.

By comparison with them, Trevor and Rosemary might appear to be a 'typical' clergy couple, yet their parishioners might be surprised to know how hard the road to ordination had been. They are in their early thirties with two young children. They live in a northern industrial town, which grew up from a series of pit villages, though the mines are now all closed. Local roots are very deep and so are the feuds of the past. A certain lack of confidence breeds a kind of bravado in what still appears to be a male-dominated society.

Church congregations are relatively large and there is a great sense of belonging. There seems to be plenty of 'religion' though some have been heard to question whether it is altogether Christian. The clergy play an important role but a latent anti-clericalism keeps them on their mettle. The vicar is seen mainly from the parishioners' point of view and even other clergy tend to regard him as having begun life at ordination!

Trevor grew up in a similar area. He actually had the experience of coming to faith when he was fifteen. He began to think very deeply about ordination and talked to the careers teacher at school about it. She took it very seriously but he said 'It was a shock to Mum.' Time went by and he drifted along, left school, tried his hand as an apprentice butcher and finally joined the police force in a nearby city. He had known Rosemary since they were teenagers. She left school at eighteen to work in a laboratory. By the time they got married they had both become very slack and had virtually lost their faith (backsliding is the term they use). She was the vicar's daughter. With three sisters and a brother she said she sometimes felt 'like the black sheep'.

Independence and their marriage, with both bringing in a good income, meant that for the first time Rosemary 'had some money to spend and was not constantly wearing secondhand clothes'. She was really delighted to feel she was a private person at last. However, marriage had other effects on them. They both took their vows very seriously. They found that they were turning back to God and returned to worship at church, where they became involved as caring members of the local congregation. After two and a half years 'bells starting ringing', to quote Rosemary. They had quite a long struggle before they came jointly to the decision that Trevor must take the first step to talk to somebody about his renewed feeling that God was calling him to be ordained.

Rosemary's father had moved to be vicar of another parish before their marriage. They said he continued to be a loving father, did not push or interfere but sat on the sidelines, wisely leaving it all to them and God. Occasionally, Rosemary found herself assailed by thoughts of 'having nothing again' and losing the freedom which their lifestyle had given them so far, especially the privacy and the shared time-off together. She rather dreaded renewed parochial expectations.

Trevor found the whole business of asking his superiors for a reference for the selection conference quite traumatic. He was afraid the police would think he had gone soft. That would have been even more embarrassing if he had not been recommended after all. They eventually had to face six years before he was finally ordained deacon. He was assigned to the Aston Training Scheme for two years, to catch up on his academic qualifications, before going to theological college. Rosemary and Trevor eventually went there together, sure that they were right to be leaving their old life behind.

Looking back on his previous experience as a policeman, Trevor feels that it has given him more, not less understanding of the society in which the Church serves. He had seen 'the whole gamut of life from the lowest to the highest', meeting people at every level, many in circumstances of great poverty and deprivation. He believes that the gulf between the Church and people is very real. He thinks that being in the police did not make him cynical, as it does many, but gave him a sense of reality and practical compassion.

Parochial expectations of new vicars ... and wives

When a vacancy occurs, the Parochial Church

Council is invited to send representations to the patron of the living (the person responsible for finding the next incumbent), with a copy to the bishop, who will often be the patron himself. Invariably the request has a certain stereotyped inevitability. Short of actually demanding the Archangel Gabriel in person, most parishioners appear to want a man between thirty-five and forty-five, preferably married with a young family. Occasionally there is particular emphasis on the need for a single man. This is usually either because the parish has a 'high church' tradition or because the last clergy wife was so dreadful! It has even been known that a single man is preferred because the last wife was so exceptional in her kindness and generosity that it is feared she might be too hard to follow.

Other considerations almost always include the demand that the next vicar should be good with young people and able to raise money. He must — of course — be a good preacher and pastor. The suggestion that somebody in their late fifties might be their next vicar may well bring the reaction that an 'old man' is being 'dumped' on a parish. Such gifts as skills in building up relationships within the congregation, and vision about working with the wider community, do not always seem to be appreciated.

A delegation once arrived in a bishop's study with not just one but two job descriptions, the second being for the wife. When asked 'What salary are you going to pay her then?' they were reduced to embarrassed silence! In spite of plenty of evidence to the contrary, parishes still hope for a 'traditional' vicar's wife, as in the past when it was implicitly understood that she would be the first lady of the parish. She would take the chair at ladies' meetings, visit the sick and needy and run her household in a virtuous manner. The majority were seen as helpmates to their husbands with ancillary status. A particularly good example of this Victorian image can be seen in Mary Sumner, who was a vicar's wife in the Winchester diocese in the last century. She was (at the time) the unwitting foundress of the Mothers' Union. Her original idea was to bring together the mothers in her parish, to pray as a group and to give each other mutual support as they struggled to bring up their children. No doubt she would have been astonished to know that this had resulted in a worldwide organization with nearly half a million members throughout the Anglican Communion. She would also have found it difficult, from the standpoint of her day, to understand that it now includes (and seeks to cherish) divorced and unmarried mothers.

I joined the Mothers' Union out of duty, as a curate's wife. In later years I came to enjoy the opportunities it gave me to get to know other women in our parishes and the challenge of helping people to look out beyond ourselves and our church communities, to find out what has really been happening to family life today. There are still many women of all ages who are very happy and willing to fill the role of vicar's wife in such ways. There are few comparable jobs where it is possible for husband and wife to share so much. A friend of mine whose husband had been a businessman before ordination told me:

'Maurice is really interesting now. We have lots to talk about . . . I wouldn't go back to the old life for anything.'

Effect on families

Many wives are not quite so sanguine at first. Rachel went off with her husband and daughter to a residential theological college in September 1990. Before they went, she talked to me about how the family had reacted. She admitted that her immediate thought when Tom told her that he had been talking to the vicar about ordination had been 'hardly fit to repeat'. When pressed she said: 'Well, I could only think how I might not be able to deal with tramps.'

Much more positive were her other remarks. 'Personally, I think it's a real challenge. It's given us a new purpose in life . . . we certainly won't have a boring middle age.' She is a very practical person. The biggest problem was what to do about their house where they had lived all their married lives, and on which they had a fixed mortgage. Even so, she could honestly say: 'We're not bothered one iota about money. We've known what it is to be almost penniless so we can cope with that again if we actually have to.'

Rachel is one of the lucky ones. She is a good communicator and has experience as a teacher. 'I shan't mind chairing meetings if that sort of thing arises in a parish', she said. The fact that there would be opportunities to share in some of her husband's training was seen as a great bonus. In the future she looked forward to seeing more of him than she ever did in the past because, however busy, he would be based at home.

While Rachel was excited and welcoming when she heard Tom's news, in spite of her surprise, their children were not at all prepared for it. Miles decided to stay with friends to finish his 'A' levels and seemed reasonably able to cope with the 'commotion' as he put it. But Paula told me that she was 'really shocked to death . . . gob-smacked!' She had no idea at all and at first 'could only think how it would affect me'. She knew that 'everything would change . . . we've always had the same roots . . . what about my friends?' She felt that there would be a stigma and that people would laugh at her because 'Dad was going to do this weird thing at his age.'

Paula felt, though, that her parents were 'happier than they've ever been'. She was sure that her mother would cope wonderfully, as 'in spite of her mad moments she's pretty level-headed.' She professed herself to be 'not all that religious' and did not think she would be very good at being 'the vicar's daughter'. Both Rachel and Paula felt that the family had grown together with 'a closeness that wasn't there before'. They found that they had got to know each other better in the months before the time when Tom went to his selection conference and the actual packing up to go away to college, nearly nine months in all. Family discussions took place on all kinds of subjects. They all knew it would 'never be the same again'.

The huge question loomed about what kind of training Tom should have and whether the family should share in it. He was already a Reader at his church. It would be hard, but not impossible, for him to continue in his job as a chemistry teacher and attend a non-residential course. At first, Paula begged that they should all stay at home, so they would still be with people they knew for as long as possible. However, she began to change her mind when her school friends started to tease her. In the end the family decided that a residential course would be much more satisfactory for many reasons.

Difficult decisions

It is not always the case that a family can respond so readily. There will be strains on a marriage during the years of training. Whether they sell up and go to a residential college together or remain in their own home, with the ordinand away from the family for many evenings and weekends, life will not be 'normal'.

When a wife shows actual hostility or real difficulties, for instance if she is an atheist herself, it is likely that the husband will be advised to resign himself not to pursue his call, at any rate for the time being. During training, a husband is likely to develop and grow and this will make the wife feel even more alienated. The future of the husband's ministry can already be perceived as being laden with problems, as well as casting huge question marks over the marriage relationship itself. Naturally, this applies equally if the candidate is a woman with an unsympathetic husband.

I was given an illustration of a case where a Diocesan Director of Ordinands who interviews and advises prospective candidates told me how he had dreaded the result if he decided to send one man to a selection conference. If the answer was 'recommended for training' the husband would be over the moon but his wife would be depressed. If 'not recommended' the husband would be depressed but the wife would be relieved. There was a real lack of communication between the two but discussing the problem with another person helped them to a mutual decision that the time was not right and they were able to be much more open with each other as a result.

Sometimes the issues which appear to be most important (and can be very difficult) are only the tip of the iceberg. Comments such as 'But what shall we do with all our furniture?' or 'A curate's house will be too small for all our family', may be hiding much greater insecurities: losing the familiar surroundings and dreading the unknown expectations of future parishioners. The family is very vulnerable in these changed circumstances.

Many families find that the realities start when the lack of money begins to bite. When David went to college his adult children were eighteen, twenty and twenty-two. Their mother described them as 'very much distressed and affected by the change', even though they were students at the time. Their father had been a doctor and the family was used to a prosperous life. Apart from anxiety about their parents' dramatic drop in salary and how it would make life less comfortable for them, the children were upset because their mother was prepared to give up the independence of her own job with students. As they had diffi-

34

culty in selling their pleasant, large house on the south coast David and his wife, Sheila, lived apart for most of his first year of training and she continued with her work until she was able to join them. This also made their children uneasy.

In fact, Sheila says that it was their children who helped them most through those sometimes quite trying years. Their support and the family's sense of humour prevented them from getting too intense and helped keep their feet on the ground. By the time David was in his second year the children decided that this was the best thing that had ever happened to him. They also found that it was the biggest conversation-stopper at parties to announce that your father was a student!

Acceptance of change

It hardly requires a great leap of the imagination to realize that for Canon Nolloth of Beverley and Rector Edwards of Wilmslow, with whom I began this chapter, the idea of an ex-policeman or insurance salesman — or even a doctor — turned vicar would be completely incomprehensible. Their wives would find it hard to understand how anybody could be a full-time teacher, health visitor or secretary as well as a 'clergy wife'. The idea that a man might be married before ordination would be equally foreign to them. Even more extraordinary would be the possibility that a wife and family might accompany an ordinand to theological college, where women would also be training for the ministry.

However one vicar, whose own call had been a

'life' vocation, told me that even as recently as the mid-1970s his own father, a clergyman, had berated him soundly because he decided to start his training as a married man! He had already written to his fiancée during their engagement asking anxious questions about whether she would cope with life in a vicarage. In their case, it took some years to stop living in the shadow of a 'perfect' clergy mother-in-law and the guilt associated with continuous disapproval from both parents. It is true that some older clergy and their wives find it hard to understand how different many of their younger colleagues are in their attitudes and the circumstances of their family life, partly as a result of the training experienced in modern theological colleges.

I hope that the examples with which I have illustrated this chapter, both personal and otherwise, may help to show that while all other 'professions' have altered radically during this century, it sometimes seems that only the church is expected to stand still. Change is accepted in almost every other department of our lives, yet the clergy appear to be caught in a time warp in many people's minds, particularly outside the church.

The picture presented by Canon Nolloth and Rector Edwards may still be the ideal dream of some present-day congregations. No doubt, they would appear to be dependable rocks of security in the fast-moving world of today. Parishes who have embraced change with enthusiasm would find them positively old-fashioned fuddy-duddies. Modern clergy usually come from a rather different mould.

3
Of Godly Life and Sound Learning

THEOLOGICAL TRAINING AND THE EFFECT ON FAMILIES

Of course, you realize that there must be no fraternizing with parishioners. Your children must not mix. You must keep a part of your house completely separate, into which the parish will not be allowed to penetrate. At parish dances — should such events even be allowed — you must see that your husbands only dance with you or the wives of the churchwardens. It would be better if you were not seen to dance, if you do, with anybody except your husband.

This was the advice given in the early sixties to the wives of ordinands by the Principal's wife at a theological college! It makes severe and rather strange reading today. Modern wives would not find it acceptable nor would it be offered. However, it does show that some thought was being given, almost for the first time, to the fact that a number of ordinands were already married.

Presumably it was considered 'necessary' to give women some kind of preparation for their future life as clergy wives. It also supposes that they were willing to receive such counsel. One of the recipients of the above was already used to vicarage life, as she had grown up in one. She is a humorous woman and says that she, at any rate, took it all with a pinch of salt.

Others were not quite so lucky in their experiences in those days, while their husbands were training for the ministry. Modern couples in this situation rarely have to endure the hardships experienced by many of their predecessors. It was quite common for a wife not to be able to see her husband at all during termtime. One family I knew, with children of seven and five, moved from their comfortable home into a flat which they made from the three attic rooms of the near-by vicarage. Jack was 250 miles away at theological college. There wasn't much money, so he could only come home for the vacations. This put a great strain on him and his wife Maggie, as they lived apart for eight months of each of the two years of training, leaving her to shoulder most of the responsibilities.

Kitty, whose present work involves counselling, told me how she had gone to work as a resident school matron while her husband Patrick underwent his first two years of training. At the end of that time, after a miscarriage and considerable unhappiness, she got a job as a typist and they managed to arrange for her to live near the college where he was a student. Their first child was born the day after he was ordained deacon. It is not surprising that they both look back on his years as a theological student with a distinctly jaundiced view.

Clergy couples, now in their forties or possibly older, will have similar memories, maybe even worse, if they were already married before or during training, as the church seemed to give very little thought to their problems at that time.

Families and the churches facing up to change

We have already seen in the previous chapter how today's ordinands come from very varied backgrounds, tend to be older than their predecessors and are usually married. The biggest problem for them and their families is facing up to the enormous changes they will need to make before they emerge as fully-fledged clergy in dog-collars, with all that this implies.

Wives feel particularly vulnerable. Marion told me how she had dreaded both the period of training which would cause upheaval and possible unhappiness and just the thought of being a vicar's wife. She had married an airline pilot and felt threatened by the prospect of a life she would be expected to share in, which would intrude on her own privacy and her job as an air hostess. The biggest hurdle to her husband Terry was the reality of getting down to academic work after such an active job.

Joyce and Richard, who went off to college with their family of three, said that they only managed to face their new life after the first fine careless rapture, because they felt so supported by friends in their home parish and the friendship of other student families in the same boat.

It is still possible to meet people who have not realized just how much things have changed, especially if they have not had an ordinand or curate in their parish, thus having little contact with recently ordained men or women. Vicars who were single when they were students themselves often seem to be largely unaware of the large number of married students today and the problems they have. As Justin, a vicar in his late thirties, ordained as recently as 1977, said, 'Married men were a very small proportion when I was at college. Most were young and recently married so wives tended to work. Certainly, we always assumed without question that they were behind their men. Some were there without their wives so we didn't see them in that light really.' Living apart like that would be unusual today but still happens in occasional instances.

When I asked parishioners outright how many clergy ordained today would have had a previous job, I was often assured that it must be about twenty per cent at most or, if pressed, perhaps forty per cent. Some older clergy also seemed to be unaware of the real situation. The truth is that it is much nearer to seventy five per cent! However, most are still relatively young and some may have done other work for only a short time before training for the ministry.

Archbishop Runcie expressed the wish, a few years ago, that more 'life' vocations might be experienced as in the old traditional pattern, where aspiring ordinands are sent to a selection conference during their student years. After graduating they either proceed straight to theological college or in some cases, at their own request or that of the selectors, spend as much as a year gaining some other kind of experience. One of our sons, after four years at university, felt that he needed a change before continuing with academic work. He was an assistant at the Anglican Centre in Rome for six months and then spent three months in Ethiopia. Both were eye-openers in rather different ways.

There are signs of a slight movement back to this pattern, as it has been recognized that perhaps there has been too much emphasis in recent years on choosing older men and women with wide experience of life. One bishop reported that it would be rare nowadays for him to ordain anybody under the age of thirty. Few will be older than forty five. It would be a mistake to assume that married status coincides with late vocation, as there are both married and single students of all ages and at all stages.

Choices: non-residential course or college

There appears to be great variety when it comes to choosing where to train. The biggest divide is between residential colleges and non-residential courses. In the former, a course lasts three years for recent graduates (two if their degree is in theology) and two for older ordinands. The non-residential courses, which developed in the 1960s, are designed mainly for men and women over thirty who train part-time over three years, while continuing to live at home doing their normal jobs.

A family faced with the decision about which is more suitable for them has to take a number of things into account. Apart from individual problems, the main considerations are usually three-fold: the house, the present job and the age and education of children, not necessarily in that order.

The house is often very important, as it may already have taken a considerable proportion of their income in mortgage, repairs and general care and is regarded with affection as the family's home. Some wives and children feel doubly threatened by the thought of losing their familiar surroundings in addition to facing an uncertain future for the next few years.

Three moves in five years is quite a common experience for families who decide on residential training. They sell up and go to college for two years, move into a curate's house for the next three and then move again, to a second curacy, a team-vicar's post or small first living. This can be very stressful for all members of the family in different ways. The emphasis on home ownership in recent years has made this a much more fraught subject than it would have been in the past. England has the highest number of owner-occupied homes in the world, with the exception of the USA. Those ordinands who have not had a previous career will not usually expect to own property, unless they have inherited some. They are sometimes rather lacking in understanding, and are even quite critical, of the anxieties which this subject can cause among others. Lisa and Barry felt that they solved this problem by selling their home and buying another one near the theological college where Barry was a student. They and their four children lived in it during that time and they have let it to other student families since they moved into a parish. This means that they still have some security in bricks and mortar.

On the other hand, some couples admitted that giving up their property and the relief from worry about mortgage and upkeep was a wonderful experience which they welcomed as the lifting of a burden. Nigel and Ruth said they had 'thought a lot on and off about being caught up in the materialism of the modern world . . . actually getting rid of the bricks and mortar made us feel really free from all that!'

Since over sixty per cent of all women are in full- or part-time paid work, many, if not most, married ordinands will have a wife — or husband — who is working. This can be the crucial issue for some families, as the partner who is not training for the ministry will usually wish to keep their job and may not be able to find a similar post near to a residential college. Sometimes this will be the deciding factor. In addition, many people in this situation feel that they have a long-standing commitment to their place of work. They may not relish being the 'spouse' in a residential situation, which makes their position much more obvious than if the ordinand in the family is doing a local course and they can carry on with their life in a more normal way as far as the outside world is concerned. Naturally, there are other husbands and wives who very much want to be part of the training experience, so for them the full-time residential course appears to be the only satisfactory answer. As far as the families themselves are concerned, I have heard many different reasons why their particular choice was made. Most do not seem to regret their decision and with hindsight still think they would not prefer any other possibility.

Those who elect to do the part-time three-year local course have to weigh up the different problems which this will present to the family. Jackie described how she had felt about accepting that it would mean much less time relaxing with her husband Geoff, not only because she already had a full-time teaching job but also because, in their case, she was the ordinand, training to be a woman deacon. She said: 'I had to set aside time to read, prepare written work and spend one night a week going to lectures. I was quite lucky as it wasn't far to travel but some people had really long journeys. We went through it all together before I started because it meant I had to be away nine weekends a year on courses as well and Geoff was told he could come to two of them with me, which he did after plenty of pleading on my part!' Some do not find the experience at all easy. Dorothy said that she found the strain 'really terrible' while her husband was training and worried about all the travelling he had to do. She continued with her job as a secretary but added sadly that she 'coped until it was over and then had a nervous breakdown'.

Couples find that they need and usually get support during this time from their local vicar and the Diocesan Director of Ordinands. Sometimes the help required is very practical advice. Charles and Mary explained that they had a slightly delicate problem. He would return from a weekend course, full of enthusiasm and excited, to find her tired after battling with the kids on her own for the whole weekend. This led to crossed wires, as he would often be looking forward to making love to her . . . the gentle suggestion was eventually made that they should try to wait for twenty-four hours!

Once the ordinand, with his or her family, has finally decided that the local non-residential ordination course is what suits them best, the choice is determined by the area in which they live. Altogether, there are fourteen non-residential courses in the Church of England, so ordinands will hope to find one which does not involve too much travelling, in addition to all the extra work which has to be fitted in with job and family.

There are also fourteen residential theological colleges, so it would seem that when all things have been considered and practical details of family involvement examined, there is plenty of choice. However, it soon becomes apparent that this is not as wide as it might seem at first. This is because, in spite of all the advances in the Christian community over the past twenty years, a great number of colleges still seem to have fairly rigid party loyalties. The same appears to be true of those choosing between Bible colleges and theological establishments training for ministry in the Methodist, Baptist and other denominations, since people bear in mind their theological stance, whether liberal or conservative.

The principal of a non-residential course who has also been on the staff of a residential college told me that, on balance, he thought the former was the preferable option. He considered that colleges tend to be too selective in their churchmanship, producing clergy with a narrower experience and vision. While 'high flyers' tend to be among the students in colleges, the non-residential courses are composed of more solidly professional people with general ability. They meet other students from varying traditions, among them a number of men and women training for the non-stipendiary ministry (licensed to a parish or other ministry but usually retaining their normal job as well) and some courses also include students training for lay ministry. Inevitably, this mixture is not found to the same degree in most residential colleges. On the other hand, it was natural that the principals of residential courses were hot in defence of the advantages of college life, stressing the value of single-minded study and the day-to-day experience of community life based on shared ideals.

In both residential and non-residential training, there is usually considerable involvement in ecumenical activities, which is seen as increasingly necessary for ministry in the future. Some courses actually combine preparation for the ministry of both the Church of England and the Free Churches with shared lectures and seminars, while also taking part in discussions and worship with them and others, including Roman Catholics and members of the Eastern Orthodox Church.

Family life in college

Young, single people and couples where the husband is under thirty will normally go to residential colleges. Couples with pre-school children also tend to opt for this manner of training, so on the whole these colleges will have a slightly younger population than non-residential courses and the families will be much more involved in the day-to-day life of the ordinand. Women with families are more likely to train near home or on a non-residential course.

It appears to be fairly clear that some single staff and unmarried students do not always appreciate the difficulties experienced by married couples and families. One single young man told me that, after living for four years with undergraduates of his own age, his first few weeks in college were quite traumatic. Sunday lunch, with numerous small children running about, were a free-for-all which he found disconcerting. As time went on, he really enjoyed it and valued belonging to such a large family. In fact, he became the favourite 'dog' on whose back the little ones loved to have rides!

Other men and women who are, or were, single in their student days vary in their attitudes. One man whose year was mostly made up of single men said that he felt far too much attention was paid to married couples and women. A Diocesan Director of Ordinands in the Midlands told me that he thought this was probably true but perhaps it was the result of guilt about the lack of such care in the past. However, in spite of this some women still feel that they are somehow second-best.

In one college it appeared that the marrieds predominated to such an extent that there were only thirteen single students altogether. A visitor described it as being 'like a morgue' at weekends when couples and families wanted private time together. He thought that the emphasis on family involvement tended to result in a lack of sensitivity towards those on their own. However, many colleges have a special celebration of Communion on Friday nights so that all the students can be together before the weekend. This contrasts oddly with Sunday mornings when colleges are even more deserted as most students are out 'on placement' taking services in local parishes.

Buildings and academic courses by themselves, however important, do not constitute a community. Invariably, in my visits to colleges and in listening to people who were still students or had recently left, there tended to be much more emphasis on personal relationships than anything else, One young curate, looking back, wrote to me: 'Traditionally, it seems, people are meant to complain about theological college. For me, however, they were a very happy three years. I enjoyed the academic work and the pastoral experience. But above all I valued the experience of community (however difficult it was at times).'

Romance is not lacking either. College staff told me with great pleasure of various pairs who left college engaged or married. John and Pat celebrated their wedding in the college chapel at the end of their training, were ordained together and now serve as curates in the same team in a town ministry. 'What better preparation could we have had for married life and ministry', said John, 'than to have been students together, sharing our faith and ideals.'

Housing problems

I have already mentioned the basic problems which

have to be faced during decision-making beforehand. It can be quite a shock when the move is actually completed.

Fiona, the wife of a professional man, with two young children of school age, spoke with distaste of the 'grotty, disgusting house' which they rented from their college in the Midlands. She looked back with longing to her 'beautiful, detached house with its lovely garden'. Her husband's vocation had, in her eyes, led to loss of status. The family's relations also seemed to regard them in this light, so there was negligible support from them as they showed little understanding of their needs.

As a complete contrast, I remember Laura, a trained lawyer, at a theological college in a university city. She referred to her first year of marriage with her husband, Roger, as 'indescribably happy'. It coincided with his final year before ordination. They lived in a cottage belonging to the college and enjoyed relative privacy, especially appreciating his long breaks between terms. Both were members of the same parish where they grew up and had caring parents in the background. These two examples, Fiona and Laura, epitomize the tremendous variety which exists, in age, experience and circumstances, within the same communities.

The practical acceptance of living in housing which, in most cases, has not been chosen personally is seen by some (and certainly by college staff) as part of the preparation for parish life in the future, particularly for living in a curate's house when first ordained. In the past, perhaps, there has been too little care over housing students' families. More recently it has been taken seriously. A good example of this is at Ripon College, Cuddesdon, where a new block was opened in 1990 specially for this purpose.

Standard of living

Many families experience a tremendous culture shock, particularly with regard to the change in their standard of living. Some said that it took the whole of the first term, from September to Christmas, a few even said two terms, to get used to living on so much less, combined with a sense of having lost command of their own lives and the complete change in their actual day-to-day activities.

Teenage children told me how they were aware that things were tight. Some resented the fact that they could no longer have the kind of clothes or presents which they had taken for granted in the past. Parents told me how sorry they sometimes felt to have to say 'No' when a child had to have what they regarded as inferior sports equipment or, more seriously, when they felt that they were not able to provide really necessary articles of clothing. On the whole, these restrictions on spending seem to be managed very well. Sixteen-year-old Patsy said 'I think it does worry Mum quite a bit but she has never let it affect us.'

When it comes to larger questions of finance, some couples do genuinely find it hard to manage on the grants available, especially when the partner who is not training has no salary. However, many spoke very warmly of the help given by various trusts and the *Church Times* 'Train a Priest' (TAP) fund money gathered entirely from contributions from readers during Lent each year. Some mature students told me that while they did not mind doing without, at times resentment built up because they felt they were in a position where they had to 'beg' for money. Others said that filling in innumerable forms wore them down. When I dared to suggest to one group that this might give them some idea of what it must be like to be unemployed and dependent on the state for money (a situation which is endemic in some parishes), I did not feel the comment was very well received.

Some wives feel aggrieved because they would rather not work but are given little option by their dioceses. Jean, a nurse living with her husband in a residential college in the north, had been told that she should avoid having children during his training, as she would be expected to provide most of the money for their upkeep. As some colleges encourage young couples to have babies while they are there this can be a cause of conflict and frustration. In contrast there are a number of middle-aged couples who end up better off than they have ever been. A young curate told me ruefully about how he and his contemporaries had resented the large cars and comparatively affluent lifestyle of some of the older students who had sold houses or were in receipt of redundancy payments.

Among married students there appear to be three categories, as far as wives who are living in college are concerned. Young wives with children form a distinct group, with babies and toddlers dominating their lives. Most of them seem to enjoy the proximity of other young families. They meet for coffee and mutual support, arrange outings and take part in discussion groups.

At the other extreme, there are wives of all ages who have full-time jobs. Some of these, including Penny who was a solicitor and Tina who worked in the DSS, expressed the feeling that they were very much 'on the outside' and unable to participate in their husbands' training, although others in the same position seemed to be a good deal more involved.

Wives who have older children but are not working seem to have the greatest opportunity for sharing in the life of the ordinands. They can go to most lectures if they wish, and many do so. One wife told me that the only bar to her total enjoyment of all this was that she felt guilty because so many other wives were not equally free to share it.

Teenagers seem to weather the change remarkably well. Louise and Emma said that it had been absolutely marvellous to see their parents 'out of the mould . . . even helping Dad to cope with writing essays . . . he hadn't a clue about English — he was an accountant before!' Younger children adjust easily in most instances and are soon assimilated into schools which are used to having children from the colleges, coming from all over the country. A mother told me that her eight-year-old son had been quite surprised when he confided in his friend, 'My Dad's going to be a vicar', to be told 'Oh, so is mine!' An older boy, looking back said: 'I really loved it at college. It's made me feel that other people are rather narrow after the experience I've had and the different people I've met.'

Preparing for parish life

Many colleges have cell groups, some involving parents and children. In addition to praying together and meeting for serious discussion, these may also involve joint holidays and weekend outings. These groups are encouraged to keep in touch after ordination. Counselling and advice are available for individuals and couples and they can take part in courses run by psychologists. When I asked one wife who had previously been a student counsellor if she had been used much personally, she laughed as she replied: 'In the college where we were, *everybody* thought they were counsellors!'

There appears to be great variation in the approach to community worship. In some colleges there is a definite rule about regular attendance in the college chapel. In others much is left to individual choice although most students are expected to have a personal director for their spiritual growth. Naturally, spouses are not required to join in to the same extent but many wish to do so.

One member of staff remarked that as most clergy are likely to find themselves on their own for a large part of their ministry, this discipline needs to be stressed early. Perhaps the most disconcerting and depressing reply I received from one couple when I asked about spiritual formation was 'Well, there was a course on Christian Spirituality but it was rather looked down on.'

They said that the emphasis throughout had been on 'success' — in preaching, pastoral care, administration. Only once had they heard a sermon on the subject of failure. Experience in parishes of different kinds, being on placement during vacations or even for a whole term, is thought to be helpful but is hardly the real thing. Stan, a former miner, who had spent a month in a suburban parish, said that he was 'tired out with having to speak to so many people!'

The extent to which theological training of any kind actually prepares ordinands for their future life in parishes seems to be debatable. It depends greatly on the attitudes of the men and women themselves and their families. The care and interest of academic and pastoral staff is also extremely important.

Living at home may seem in some ways to be a softer option than packing up and going off to college but wives and families find the situation very hard in some cases. The reality of what it will all mean often does not begin to dawn until rather late, usually at the beginning of the third year, when the dioceses start to ask questions about the kind of parish which might be most suitable. The family which has stayed in their own house and continued to worship in their familiar parish church will be faced with a sudden move at the end. Their world will not have changed perceptibly until then.

Families who have lived together in college may be accused of living in a fantasy world, but at least most of them will have got used to the idea of moving and managing on less income, with a lower standard of housing and the prospect of a curate's house.

I was assured that however much a student family is advised in advance of the pitfalls awaiting them, they can't usually understand the reality until they have actually moved into a parish. A college lecturer, reflecting on the attitude towards the future of the 'typical' ordinand (surely no such person can exist?) summed it up as 'naïve optimism coupled with anxious pessimism'.

4
Set Them
Among Your People

LIVING IN THE VICARAGE

All over England there are large, stone houses, often with spacious grounds, lawns, trees and shrubberies, gracious reception rooms and provision for resident maids in the attics. They are usually situated next to the parish church, in villages or market towns and bear on their gates the legend 'The Old Vicarage' or 'The Old Rectory'.

Nowadays, almost without exception, these are the homes of rich industrialists, successful authors or well-heeled 'yuppies'. Others have been converted into nursing homes, conference centres or luxury hotels. Examples which come to mind include St Nicholas' Vicarage in Great Yarmouth, where five maids were employed before the First World War and Ecton, near Northampton, which has become a diocesan retreat house.

These houses are a legacy of the past, when many parsons came from upper- or middle-class families with plenty of money (although there were always some who were poor). Victorian clergy quite often added a wing, at their own expense, to accommodate their many children or extra servants. Some older clergy and their wives tell tales of appalling conditions, managing frightful kitchens and living in large rooms which were impossible to heat. They also remember being paid quarterly. As one told me: 'At the beginning of the quarter we felt so rich that we could almost go out and buy a grand piano! By the end of three months we were usually in dire straits, keeping up appearances but almost starving.' A prosperous man now in his fifties remembers how, when he first met his wife, a vicar's daughter, he was shocked to find that the family lived mainly in one room in the winter, huddling round the fire to keep warm.

Popular images of vicarage life, especially on TV or in novels, still tend to portray the stereotype of the big house, along with the bumbling vicar, cucumber sandwiches with tea on the lawn, a sweet-natured wife in the drawing room and the cook in the kitchen. But since the mid-1970s the Church of England has progressively divested itself of most of these large mansions, helped considerably by the Church Commissioners, who support and enable building and many other needs of the Church of England with money which comes mainly from investments and property. Modern vicars are more likely to live in trim, brick-built, detached houses with central heating and manageable gardens.

The ideal is to provide a family sitting-room and dining room which are also big enough to accommodate meetings from time to time, a modern kitchen and garage. There should be at least four bedrooms, providing 'sleeping for six people', a bathroom and sometimes an additional shower room. In some vicarages the study is separate from the rest of the house and may have its own entrance and doorbell.

It seems to be difficult for anybody who has not personally experienced living in a vicarage to appreciate what it actually feels like. Parishioners and occasional visitors are influenced by their own perceptions and prejudices, even if they know the vicarage family quite well (and this can include relatives). The lack of personal privacy appears to be the greatest burden and was high on the agenda of most families who talked to me. 'Just to be able to lie in as long as we like, trail round in our dressing gowns for half the morning and enjoy being really free to do our own thing on our day off . . . to stay here in the house without the doorbell ringing or the undertaker phoning . . . that would be a real treat!' Carol, whose dream this was, told me that a parishioner had once turned up wreathed in smiles, saying, 'I know it's your day off but you won't mind ME calling because today I've just come as a friend.' No wonder many clergy couples feel they have to go out to have a real day off because there is no guarantee that they can enjoy peace and privacy at home. Some wives told me that they actually put up notices about it but unfortunately this tends not to be very well received or understood.

Carol also remembered the bank holiday when a young couple came to ask her husband, Frank, to christen their baby on the following Sunday. Although the house was full, as both sets of grandparents had come for the birthday of one of his own children, Frank was polite and invited them in but had to explain that it would not be possible since there would be a confirmation on that day. He also said that he would wish to talk to them beforehand about what baptism should mean in terms of commitment in the future and asked them to come back the next day. They were filled with consternation, having taken 'the church part' for granted, and informed him that the party was arranged already and all their relatives were coming specially! After they had left, Frank and Carol managed to laugh at the attitude towards them and the church generally, having become used to such incidents. However, their parents were quite shocked, both at the details of the visit and — perhaps even more — at the intrusion into their privacy on a national holiday.

Family life in this country has become considerably more self-contained in recent years, with TV sets in bedrooms, personal computers and all the technical innovations to be found in modern homes. Professor Laurie Taylor once said in 'Personal View' (broadcast on 21 and 22 October 1988 on the BBC World Service) that we have become 'singularly poor at making friends', having very little to do with our neighbours. He concludes that 'in this massive retreat into the home we close the door against the world.' This is the direct antithesis of vicarage life, as I and most clergy families I know understand it. It never occurred to me, when I was a vicar's wife, not to answer the phone or the door. I always knew that it might be somebody in distress, perhaps sick or dying. It usually turned out to be something extremely banal, such as a message from the organist or a question about the time of a service. It came as quite a shock to me to discover nonclergy friends who had ex-directory telephone numbers (usually for very good reasons), as our house had of necessity to be accessible to everybody.

This accessibility is probably greatest where the vicarage is situated next to the church. Relatively few parishes now have vergers, so the vicar and his family often find themselves doing chores — constantly producing keys for all and sundry and being responsible for opening up the parish hall in time for meetings or the vestry for choir practice. It often falls to them to turn on the church heating, usually oil or gas nowadays, but in some cases there are still ghastly old coke-fired boilers.

I remember some very well-heeled friends arriving unexpectedly one Saturday afternoon to see the parish to which we had just moved. They finally ran us to earth in the church, where we were cleaning, covered in dust and very filthy. Up till then I think they had imagined that vicars spent their time in their study or the pulpit. The fact was that the church had been neglected for years in spite of the fact that most of the parishioners' own homes had beautifully stoned doorsteps and shone with brasso and polish. It was not long before there was a proper cleaning rota — perhaps we shamed them into it.

Blessed interruptions

I used to pull a face sometimes when Michael referred to 'blessed interruptions', St Teresa's pious description of the many unexpected callers of various kinds who arrive at the vicarage, including tramps. These have always been an

60

expected and accepted feature of vicarage life. We are told by St Paul to 'be given to hospitality'. On the whole vicarage families interpret this not only by entertaining parishioners and others in various ways but also in ministering to the 'gentlemen of the road' who arrive at their door. These vary considerably from old 'regulars', who may come into the kitchen for a cup of tea and something to eat, to quite young vagrants who can often be fairly frightening. The latter are more common today and are sometimes on drugs.

Elaine and Keith live in a fairly lonely rectory, set back behind the church and hidden from a busy main road. They get a great number of tramps and usually give them food rather than money, while taking care not to put themselves at risk if possible. Elaine told me about what she considers to have been her most frightening experience.

One bitterly cold February day Keith was out and I had both the children in bed upstairs with measles when the doorbell rang. Outside stood a young man, shivering with cold and looking very pathetic. He stumbled over the doorstep asking for help. At the time I felt so sorry for him that I could only feel pity, so I put him in the study and got him some food and a hot drink. He told me that he had just come out of the psychiatric ward of the local hospital and was trying to get back to his sister's home but the money she had sent for his fare had all been taken away by other patients to whom he was in debt. He became more and more strange and started to take out of his pockets dozens of pictures of Tutankhamen and mummified bodies, which he said he collected. Then he confided that he was fascinated by the thought of death.

By this time I was really terrified, desperate to go to my children but frightened that he might follow me. Somehow, I managed to creep away to the phone upstairs and rang a friend in the parish, whispering anxiously that I needed her to come. The children were asleep so I returned to the study, where my visitor seemed to be dozing. After a while he suddenly got up and placed himself between me and the study door, becoming more and more excited and frantically waving his horrible pictures at me. Just when I was almost ready to scream with fear, Keith arrived home and took over the situation. I have never been so terrified in all my life. It made me very wary about opening the door to anybody for a long time.

Most callers do not have this effect. They are usually known, familiar people who are often friends and prove to be very supportive. I have many personal memories, in common with most clergy wives, of great kindness and understanding. This was shown both in practical ways such as babysitting and down-to-earth help when my children were small (the churchwarden's wife once took off a whole bucketful of my baby's nappies and returned them fresh and clean!) and in sympathetic care for me as an individual. On one occasion I remember opening the door to the Mothers' Union committee and bursting into tears. They recognized my tired state, were very practical and put the kettle on!

Daphne, a rather shy young wife in her early thirties, described how the parish rallied round her husband and three young children when she had rheumatic fever. She said: 'Nothing was too much trouble. Tony was taken to school and met in the afternoons, the small ones were looked after during the day, Maurice was liberally supplied with food and I was heaped with good wishes and flowers.' Her husband said that they had felt they were supported on a constant cloud of prayer. In another parish I was told that when the vicar's wife went into hospital to have a hysterectomy the women of the parish organized a chain of people to deliver two meals each day for the three men in the household. This was kept up for some time after their own 'housekeeper' returned.

There are times when people might prefer to be a little more private, such as the first few weeks of pregnancy. When I was expecting my first baby we moved just as I was experiencing rather acute symptoms, feeling sick and not looking very well. There was no way I could hide my secret and for the next seven months I was subjected to constant remarks, such as 'Mind how you go . . . look after that baby of ours.' It was all well meant and quite humorous but for anyone more shy than I am it could be very embarrassing. In my case, it meant that when I was expecting my next baby (fortunately with no distressing symptoms) Michael and I decided that this was to be our 'private' baby and we did not tell anybody until it was really necessary! I heard later that the gossips in the parish had put this down to the fact that I must be 'ashamed' that they were so close. When our daughter was born within a year of our next move, I was amused (and made thoughtful) when a forthright man in the congregation told me: 'It's the best thing that's happened in this parish for years. None of us can remember a baby being born at the vicarage. Now we know that you're really human!'

Meg, a very smart wife in a suburban parish in the Midlands, told me that when she ventured to say at a parish pantomime that her husband was not really a 'leg' man, a surprised parishioner replied, 'Oh, I never thought I'd hear a vicar's wife say that. I've always thought of clergy as a-sexual somehow!'

This points up the assumptions which are still around about clergy couples. People seem to feel more secure if they can remove them from normal life and experience and put them on a pedestal. They often assume that it is easier to stay married in a vicarage, perhaps unaware of the stresses which are caused by living at the hub of the wheel. I have always maintained that more 'dirt' (such as real poverty and desperate family situations) comes over a vicarage doorstep than any comparable home. 'How are we meant to find space for each other when we spend so much time helping other people to stay together?' asked a middle-aged wife in a suburban parish in the South West. Her husband added that on the previous evening a hysterical woman had turned up during their meal and hurled herself at him, screaming that her husband was having an affair with another member of the congregation.

Ordained men and women and their partners

find themselves used by people who put them into awkward situations. Sometimes this can arise through tale-telling, varying from apparently harmless asides to downright maliciousness. It can be hard to remain aloof from the gossip and tittle tattle which sometimes goes on in the vicarage kitchen. There can be few clergy wives who have not suffered from the threat (real or imagined) posed by other women in the parish. Liz, a highly intelligent teacher, told me how she had felt when her children were little:

> There I was, mother of four girls under seven, struggling with the house, phone, doorbell, everything . . . there he was, my holy workaholic, with a stream of beautifully dressed, well-manicured, middle-aged women, most of them with their own cars and — the one thing I hadn't got — plenty of time. They seemed to stream through my front door as though I were the maid, making me feel that I was an uninteresting young wife forever knee-deep in children. They adored HIM and obviously thought that they would be much better clergy wives than I was.

She admitted to a certain wicked pleasure when she emerged as a professional woman, holding down a good job, after her last child went to school.

Culture shock

Culture shock, already referred to as a condition experienced by families in theological colleges, seems to be a fairly common experience, especially for those who move into areas entirely unlike the one they grew up in. Colin and Anna, a young couple living in a flat in a high-rise block in a densely populated, poor outer-city estate in the North East, said they were happy to be sharing the same living conditions as the parishioners round them. At the same time, as they had become aware that two incomes came into their flat while most other tenants were living on the dole, Anna had given up her job in the city for a part-time, more home-based one which gave her more time to share with her husband and to be around in the parish.

They had both come from middle-class homes, where it was taken for granted that you worked at school, did 'O' and 'A' levels and hoped to go to university. This had been their own experience. They had taken time to realize that the whole ethos of the estate was totally alien to any such ideas. There, children were lucky to finish school at all. They rarely had any expectations of themselves, nor did their parents have any for them. Families lived from day to day, often with both parents out of work and adult children living at home with nothing to do. The pawn shop was in great demand as few had any savings and they blew any money that they did get. Balancing all this there was a very supportive, accepting community with extended family networks and a high rate of illegitimacy, widely tolerated and regarded as normal. As Anna said, 'It's all rather far removed from college flower arranging!'

In a run-down but still expensive part of a southern city, a vicar's wife told me how upset she had felt when some young mothers in the pram group had wanted to take photographs of her house to show their friends because they thought it was so 'lovely and posh'.

A middle-aged couple moved from the South, via a theological college in the Midlands, to a similar situation near a large northern city. Betty found herself without a job and a car of her own for the first time for years. She said that at first she couldn't get over the despair of the estate. She and her husband lived in a very pleasant, modern vicarage, quite the largest house in the whole area, standing out like a sore thumb in a sea of mean terraces and tower blocks. Initially, they felt so desperate about the conditions around them that they asked one another, 'Where's God in all this?' In time, they made God's presence very real to people through their own accepting attitudes, their open house and their prayerful dedication to the needs of those of the whole community.

Such things as holidays abroad became a thing of the past because most of their parishioners never had a holiday at all. They had dropped many thousands of pounds in income and lived, carefully, on the clergy stipend but they felt that the people round them regarded them as rich and, because some remnants of their past comfortable life were still present in the furnishings of their vicarage, considerably richer than they actually were!

This approach costs a family dearly in terms of their own privacy and is certainly not possible for all to sustain. Some families have found that they cannot cope with these conditions and end up barricading themselves in, especially if they have been burgled several times by people who may be on drugs, as is frequently the case.

It can be equally disturbing for clergy to experience the move from such a parish to a country living, where the expectations will be very different. Hilary, used to being on Christian name terms with everybody, with a vicarage constantly invaded by all and sundry and a close network of friendly parishioners in an urban setting, found the contrast really upsetting. She had problems when people referred to her husband as 'The Rector' and found that she was now 'The Rector's Wife'. People did not regard her house as a place where they could drop in and for a time she found herself in a state of isolation. The village was very dead during the week as a large number of parishioners commuted and some houses were empty for long periods, having become second homes for city-dwellers. Because they only had one car she felt very cut off as public transport was minimal.

There were other problems for her husband Chris, who was responsible for three other villages in addition to the one where they lived. This was the first time two of these parishes had not had their own parson living in their midst for a thousand years. They found the prospect of sharing a priest very unwelcome and, as Chris said, they showed it! 'Even though they understood with their heads they found it hard to accept with their hearts.' Hilary sometimes felt she was 'the catalyst for all the warring factions: the four separate PCCs, the churchwardens, everybody's problems, nobody seeming to realize that I might have any of my own', as she constantly manned the telephone.

Sundays were fairly exhausting, as Chris travelled from village to village. At first Hilary tried to go with him to the services in each of the churches but eventually she opted for the one near her home, where she could attend regularly. She got to know members of the congregation and came to enjoy the very different pace of country life after her previous experience in the city. Another wife spoke to me of accompanying her husband to services on one day at 8.00 am, 9.00 am, 10.00 am, 11.00 am and 11.30 am. She was a very gregarious person and loved meeting people.

Families with children tend to have problems in the country if there are no local schools. Some wives manage to run a car and have a job, in which case it will probably be the husband who spends long hours alone. Although this type of ministry appears totally uninviting to many people, I met some who seem to be very contented and fulfilled in these circumstances. A recent report, *Faith in the Countryside* (September 1990), abounds with information on this kind of area, where there are more sheep than people.

At the other end of the scale, there are what used to be called the 'plum' parishes. These are mainly to be found in the well-heeled suburbs or the stockbroker belt. Incumbents in these places are unlikely to be troubled by any anxieties that they might have superior wealth, better education or similar problems as far as their parishioners are concerned. They may live in beautiful houses but as they will usually be con-

siderably worse off materially than their neighbours, they will need to be good managers. As
Madge, a very smart wife whose husband is vicar
of an 'up-market' parish said, 'It's perishing cold
in the winter but I've worked hard to keep our
heads above water and keep up appearances.'

However, this type of parish is likely to be more
accepting of 'working' clergy wives than most
others, since there will be a fairly high proportion
of professional women already taking their own
jobs seriously. The vicar's family will also tend to
find friends who share their background and interests and may hope for some intellectual stimu-
lation. Nevertheless, despite these possible
advantages, it is interesting that a fairly high proportion of families say that they have been happier in working-class parishes, working alongside
unemployed and deprived people. A mother who
was expecting her fourth baby rather late in life,
said that she could have had ten prams — there
were so many generous offers of help — whereas
in the rich parish where her husband had been
curate when she had her first baby there had been
what she termed 'polite interest'.

Harry and Marjorie, a gentle, middle-aged couple,
explained with wry humour how they had tried
hard to live a 'simple' life in a very rich part of the
south, and commented that they seemed to be the
only people in the parish who did not employ a gar-
dener! The Parochial Church Council were so anxious about the elderly state of the vicar's car (or
ashamed, he thought) that they tried to persuade
him to let them buy him a new one.

On the whole there appears to be a fairly high

rate of satisfaction with the accommodation provided in vicarages, but less with that for curates and their families. Jobs are sometimes refused on account of the house, if it is thought to be unsuitable for the family's needs. This freedom of choice is considered by many people to be a privilege which the clergy enjoy in much greater measure than most other people. At its simplest, it would seem that they can choose a house to accommodate four, five or more in comfort, in whatever part of the country they prefer and move when it suits them, enabling them to consider their own commitments, their spouse's job and their children's schooling. In theory it also means that clergy should be able to experience plenty of variety during their ministry, moving from town to country, from suburb to market town and vice versa, in a way that is rarely possible in any other job, though of course it is rarely as easy as this.

Job security and housing

However, the job security which can be taken for granted by the clergy is almost unique, and all the more to be envied in a world where even those with apparently rock-solid positions in prominent firms know that they can be made redundant at any time. Very few in today's society dare refuse when they are offered a move, knowing that there may never be another opportunity. The vicar of a prosperous northern parish told me how he had just spent two hours with a family, in a lovely house with a Jag in the drive and four children at a private school. The father had been given a week's notice at the age of fifty-four as his firm was going into liquidation. They were desperate, with no prospect of alternative employment which would enable them to continue paying their mortgage or the school fees. Their vulnerability made the parish priest 'feel powerless to help them in any practical way and also guilty myself because I knew that this could never happen to my own family. The bishop has asked me to move twice but it didn't suit us to at the time. After all, I can stay here till I'm seventy if I want to . . . I have the freehold and I have my house!'

The tied houses which vicars and their families live in may be in Mayfair or Brixton, Wilmslow or Toxteth. They are maintained by the diocese and inspected every five years. The lack of financial responsibility for such property is sometimes envied by those who are struggling to pay mortgages, especially at times of high interest rates. Clergy families may never suffer the dread connected with buying and selling their house (see chapter 6) or the anxieties of a bridging loan. They do not have to give up their holiday because the drive needs mending or the house needs a new roof. Parishioners may feel at times that vicars do not understand the pressures on many other families in this respect because they do not experience them personally. (Although, as has been observed in earlier chapters, many more clergy nowadays have previously been owner-occupiers and some still manage to maintain a property of their own.)

There is no doubt that the subject of housing

comes very high on the agenda of most clergy families — too high, in the opinion of some older couples, many of whom told me that they think the younger clergy of today are quite spoilt in comparison with the past. One archdeacon, fairly new in his post, told me that he was astounded at the extremely high standard of modern vicarages and at the expectations of clergy wives. Since he had a son struggling with a young family and a high mortgage he said that he sometimes found it hard to be polite when asked for expensive fittings or when he received demands that a damaged wall should be repaired immediately.

On the other hand, the Church of England principle of living over the shop means that some families feel they pay the high price of accessibility. The institution of the parish office has become much more common during the last twenty years. This is normal practice in North America as our family discovered as long ago as 1975 when we went to California on a parish exchange thirty miles from San Francisco. Michael worked office hours next to the church, a mile away from the privately-owned vicar's house where we lived for six weeks. Nobody either came to the house or telephoned there on parish business except in a real emergency. All that went to the parish office. I had no sense of being a clergy wife. As I remember that situation and a subsequent visit to the Niagara diocese in Canada in 1985, I feel personally that it tends to lead to greater isolation for the vicarage family. It seems to me that the office should be the place for typewriter, photocopier, word processor (and possibly the fax machine), where basic clerical work may be done. It is a rather impersonal setting in which to offer help to a couple whose marriage is in trouble or to talk to young men or women who feel they may have a vocation to the ministry. The vicarage study should be the place for that.

Owning your own house

At times there are calls for all vicarages to be sold and a housing allowance to be available instead, which would enable clergy to buy their own homes. The last time this was considered in any serious way, the Church Commissioners concluded that the money invested from such a sale would be insufficient to fund mortgages. A vociferous vicar's wife in the South who thought that 'clergy should be paid a suitable wage so they could choose' was gently reminded by other wives in the group discussing the subject that none of them could even begin to think of purchasing the houses they lived in. Some might be worth half a million on the open market!

This highlights one of the problems which house-owning clergy would face. It would make moving much more difficult — the incumbent who might care to be a vicar in Mayfair would doubtless find it impossible to purchase a house there if the one he was trying to sell was in Brixton. In some parishes nothing might be available at all, particularly in inner-city areas and the picture of commuting vicars (already seen to be unpopular in country areas) seems to go against the very nature of the priestly vocation to be 'servant and shepherd among the people to whom he is sent', as it says in the Ordination service. In one parish we were the only professional couple actually living within the parish boundaries, as doctors, teachers and others all chose a more salubrious part of the town. We felt we needed to be part of our patch. In many inner-city areas the clergy are among the few people who really know the scene, as was clear during the Toxteth riots of 1981, whereas people like social workers and probation officers often live well away from their work.

Accommodation for Curates

The temporary nature of accommodation for curates and their families sometimes causes problems as this is the responsibility of the parish. In 1956 our first home was a flat composed of four rooms on the first floor of a house which was occupied by the owners in the summer. They happened to be an exceptionally unpleasant family, with an alcoholic mother who was less than cordial to us. We shared the front door with them and the couple who lived on the top floor. None of the flats were self-contained so it was wise not to run out of the bedroom half-dressed in case we met anybody going past in the corridor on their way upstairs. There was always trouble about our callers, especially the youth club. We had no telephone. We paid rent, unlike almost all our contemporaries. This is not intended to be a sob story; it simply illustrates the fact that our expectations were not very high. We had three gloriously happy years there. Our parents were perhaps too polite at the time to tell us what they actually thought!

A curate moving into a parish today would normally find better conditions than I have just outlined, although it can still be a shock to a family when they actually see the house the parish expects them to live in. Equally, a parish which has been used to single curates may find the prospect of housing a married man with three teenage children somewhat daunting!

Most people who told me about their experiences appear to have managed reasonably well, though I did hear occasional horror stories, particularly about houses not being at all ready for occupation. It is not unknown for curates to make a humorous bid for attention. Malcolm, who had been a university lecturer before he was ordained, requested an indoor cloakroom as his curate's house, in a big city parish, had an outside loo. When nothing happened, he invited the parochial Church Council to a party on a cold January night and gave them plenty to drink: they got the message!

However, Bob and his family found their tiny house in a prosperous parish so cramped and unsuitable that he was not inclined to be so tactful when asked by the churchwardens if they needed anything. He suggested that one of them, with their wife and two children, might like to exchange houses with him. By way of contrast, Dinah and Nick, in a parish in the South East, reported that it was 'excellent for the two of us. A three-bedroomed detached house on a new estate with a reasonable-sized garden. The parish is very good about paying for repairs and upkeep.' The same size house for another family had rather more disadvantages as they commented 'the dining room has to double as a study and the kitchen is too small to eat meals in. With two teenagers (boy and girl) and no spare room for relatives or friends, we do feel rather cramped especially as we came from a much larger house.'

Ann, whose husband served in what she described as 'a mainly affluent residential area', commented:

> The parish has been very generous with regard to housing. The curate's house was in a poor state of repair but . . . there was time for a complete programme of renovation — new kitchen, new bathroom, redecoration etc., which we have very much appreciated. We are aware how lucky we are, as a family of five to be living in such spacious, pleasant surroundings.

'How many jobs welcome you to a new home with cards, flowers and a larder full of food?' asked one young wife, full of gratitude. Others are not so lucky. Some have to learn the hard lesson that on the whole parishioners are not particularly interested in their past, expect them to settle down fairly quickly, continue the practices of their predecessors and relate to them. This can be hard on a family who may feel that their previous experiences were worthwhile.

However, in most cases people are usually very anxious to make their new vicar or curate and his or her family welcome and many find a loving, helpful community around them. Unlike lay families, who have to start from scratch to build up their own network of friends without the assistance of a parochial base, they will usually find themselves presented with an immediate extended family, for better or worse.

Vicarage Children

The children who grow up in vicarages share the same array of advantages and disadvantages as their parents, although they are fortunate, for the most part, in not being as self-conscious about them. In meeting a good number, of different ages, I formed the opinion that they are generally rather a pleasant bunch of people! Certainly many are easy to talk with, being used, as one said, to 'opening the door to anybody and everybody, from tramps to bishops'.

They are realistic about life, having understood from an early age that life is not perfect and can never ultimately be lived in a private way. They naturally inherit some of the attitudes of their parents towards parishioners, as I discovered from listening to them. Jimmy, aged twelve, smiled as he told me how he had seen an old lady with her hair in curlers, rolling drunkenly round their garden on Christmas night. 'Poor old Dad had been up for Midnight Mass the night before so he was dog tired, but he went and got her in. We wouldn't have expected anything else.'

Children from vicarages with 'open doors' said how much their friends liked coming round and that they enjoyed knowing so many people. One nine-year-old wrote to me that 'it's nice because you have lots of aunties and uncles'. However, her elder brother, who incidentally gave me two accounts — one headed 'Totally Truthful!' — said, 'In a vicarage there's just no peace. Sometimes its quieter and less busy in school.' Their older, newly-married sister was more positive. She said that she had never found the life 'ordinary or boring'. Looking back, she remembered how the family 'often had to share our parents with foster children, boys from an approved school and children who needed a holiday. I did at times resent this but now I realize how much I admire my parents for what they did and know that I did benefit and learn a lot from these experiences.' She thought that growing up in a vicarage was hardly what she could call 'a normal upbringing' but described it as 'happy and unselfish' and said that her friends soon understood that 'it wasn't all prayers and religion!'

Clergy children, now grown up with families of their own and usually more affluent than their parents had been, generally spoke of not having been particularly aware of financial hardship, although they realized that careful housekeeping had been exercised. One said that 'every reel of cotton had to be calculated but food was always plentiful but plain.' The same man, now a vicar himself, was grateful that he had only known big houses in his youth, usually had his own room and had valued the space afforded in their large family home. His own modern vicarage, pleasant though it is, makes it harder to keep open house as his parents had done, if the family is to enjoy any privacy.

Another vicarage son said:

I had a very happy, stable childhood anyway. I recognize now that Dad was around a lot more than was true for many of my contemporaries; that Mum was there (but then she didn't work really outside the home much). The feel of the thing is a lot more difficult to pin down . . . people coming in and out of the house, having some basic understanding of confidentiality fairly early on, being very much part of a community, this last has probably been the most influential part for me, as has the fact that we are a very close family.

When I asked him if he had felt that living in a vicarage had made him somehow 'different', he replied:

If I felt it much at the time it wasn't oppressive. I didn't consciously suffer at school from being the vicar's son. As for values — how I regarded, and had been brought up to regard, money and possessions — I was really quite proud of my early feelings about all this. The sense of detachment from things, without being negative in its attitude (I hope) is still very important in my life (and, I think, in the lives of my brother and sister).

Many spoke of the affection with which they were treated by parishioners when they were growing up. They also appreciated the presents (sometimes quite lavish) which were heaped on them. I remember personally how I was showered with gifts, including twenty-eight matinee coats, when my first baby was born! My children always had innumerable presents at Christmas and rows of Easter eggs in the spring.

There are countless stories of vicarage children who turn out to be the black sheep of the family. It is true that a good number do go into a state of revolt, about which both they and their parents may feel more guilty than they really need, simply because they are aware that others expect them to set a good example. In fact, most parents — whether clergy or lay — are likely to experience difficulties with at least some of their teenage children. There is nothing new about this. As one of my sons, then aged fifteen, put up on my kitchen wall: 'The young people of today think of nothing but themselves. They have no reverence for parents or old age; they talk as if they alone knew everything.' That was said by Peter the Hermit in AD 1247.

One occasion which my own family remembers well, was when Mary Whitehouse and her husband came to supper in our vicarage. The children were banished to the kitchen in case they disgraced us. They were annoyed at being left out so they proceeded to make such a terrible noise that I had to keep putting my head round the door, gesticulating in silent fury, which just made them even worse!

I noticed, when speaking to some of the younger children, that the subject of school seemed to crop up much more. An eleven-year-old boy said: 'You get skitted a fair bit at school.' Another, in an inner-city parish, said he got remarks if his father dropped him off in his car: 'Coming to school in a hearse then?' Other remarks were

'People don't expect you to be human', 'You can get a lot of teasing from non-Christians', 'I hate being called the vicar's kid.' Parents told me that their children were sometimes singled out by teachers. This seems to be particularly unfair and insensitive. The worst example I heard was of a child who was made to stand up and was then introduced as 'the new curate's daughter'. Children who had been away at college with their families seemed to feel this more, perhaps because they had not grown up as clergy children from the beginning. Some told me that they had preferred it when their fathers were students because there had been plenty of other children at local schools in the same situation.

Living so much in the public eye certainly has its disadvantages but every complaint and wry face was more than balanced by appreciation of the many advantages of vicarage life. I asked a number of clergy couples what other jobs they thought might make more demands on family life. Among the replies were oil-rig workers, airline pilots, long-distance commuters, sea captains and nuclear submariners.

A wife whose husband had previously been a systems analyst was able to say: 'I think our life is much better than many other people's. It's a great privilege to share in joys and sufferings. There's great variety and we're never bored. There are frustrations, moments of sadness and demands on your time but the joy of seeing God working in people's lives outweighs these.' She acknowledged, as we all do, that there are some terrible days 'when the telephone never stops, there seems to be one crisis after another, you have no time to yourself.' But she had survived all that pretty well so far and realized how supportive parishioners can be. She said, 'I called on someone the other day — a lady who is housebound and whom I hadn't seen for a while. As I was leaving, she said "I keep praying for you." I'm sure that's the secret — the friends who pray for us and we ourselves keeping in touch with God. That's how we keep going even when the pressure is on.'

5
Fellow Servants
in Christ

PARISH, COMMUNITY AND DIOCESE

In 1956, I was the only clergy wife in our area to work, in the sense of having paid employment. This was regarded by some parishioners very critically though it was possibly made more acceptable because I was teaching in a girl's grammar school which was highly respected in the town.

There were thirty-three members of staff. Thirty were single ladies and three of us were married. Two of us were curates' wives. We always sat together in break, hardly daring to mention our husbands or the fact that we had any interest in life outside school. The other teachers were mostly very pleasant, dedicated women for whom I had the utmost respect, particularly because many of them came from the generation before mine who had to choose between marriage and a career.

This meant that for the first three years of my marriage, I was constantly trying to maintain a balance between the different expectations of these two almost separate parts of my life. In spite of this, I do not remember being particularly fraught, although occasionally I felt unhappy at the implied criticism from both camps. Maybe because of this, I know that I did try assiduously to be 'a good curate's wife'! This included coming home, unless I was on duty, to get my husband's lunch and seeing that he never had to do any housework as the parishioners would definitely not have approved (nor would he in those days!).

My own background of faith and religious observance was in any case taken for granted so fortunately it meant that church attendance was no problem. However, looking back now I consider that three services on Sundays and teaching a Sunday-School class in the afternoon might seem excessive today. I ran the cake stall at the Christmas bazaar, my own rather amateur efforts notwithstanding, joined the Mothers' Union and was a member of the Parochial Church Council.

Michael's day off was on a Thursday, which happened to be early closing day. In those days this meant that literally every shop closed in the whole area. As I was free on Saturdays, the only time we shared a day off together was during my school holidays. Our transport consisted of a bicycle for the first two years (a moped for four years thereafter), on which he pedalled between two churches three miles apart. On the comparatively few occasions when we travelled together, it was on buses and trains.

If I were starting married life as a curate's wife in the 1990s, I realize that the conditions I would be likely to experience would probably be almost the exact opposite of the picture I have just outlined. I might well be the odd one out in the area if I did NOT work outside my home. Equally, if I did, especially if the job was teaching, I should

85

find myself in the majority in the staffroom as a married woman. I doubt whether I should feel obliged to attend all the church services and I should surely feel much more free to choose in which areas of parish ministry, if any, I could be most useful. I should expect at least some consideration to be given to my needs to share time with my husband so that his day off might coincide with mine or at any rate be a little flexible. These expectations would not be unusual today because it is largely accepted that many clergy wives are likely to be in paid employment.

Working wives

It is now very common for a 'typical' clergy couple to be a 'working' wife and a husband who has had a late vocation to the ministry. While I personally deplore the term 'typical', I use it here deliberately for the very reason that it has been applied so liberally in the past but with a very different image in mind: that of the 'unpaid curate' wife and the kindly, well-meaning parson with the sonorous voice.

Like any other modern husband and wife, clergy have to consider the relative stress which a wife's job may cause to their marriage and the effect on their family if they have one. However, in addition they will also need to decide the degree of her involvement in the parish, the use of the vicarage and their own privacy and opportunities for leisure time together: all this in the light of lingering images of the role of the vicar's wife, even in some of the most enlightened parishes. A number of working wives told me that they experienced a feeling of disapproval from some parishioners and occasionally from other clergy wives who were not working. I remember a conversation with a Rural Dean's wife from a northern diocese not many years ago on the subject of local wives' groups meetings. I turned cold when she said 'Well of course, I don't consider a wife who goes out to work to be a "proper" clergy wife at all. I don't bother to include them.'

In my own experience, meeting an interesting variety of wives in preparation for this book, I found a definite difference in attitude between North and South. One group in the South East assured me vehemently that this was so. Certainly the majority appeared to consider that they had an absolute right to their own careers. A similar group in the North were less determined about this, although many had jobs of their own, mostly taken up rather later after their children had all gone to school or when their husbands moved parishes.

I met a number of clergy wives who said they were only regarded as contributing properly to the household if they were doing so financially, like their contemporaries. They felt that their right to choose to stay at home had been removed by society. Young mothers are no longer asked 'Will you be going back to work?' but 'WHEN will you be going back to work?' In this respect clergy wives have more choice because in most cases they are not subject to the most dominant pressure on the finances of many lay families, that of mortgages previously arranged and dependent on two incomes.

Many of the working clergy wives I met were teachers, a profession which usually fits in well with their husbands' work. A fairly high proportion, and some of the kindest according to parishioners, were nurses. It obviously suits some couples very well and brings pleasure to both partners for the wife to have her own job. Mike, a vicar in his late forties, told me that it had brought some variety into their lives and helped his wife, Viv, 'to feel fulfilled and much more fun to live with' when she went back to work as a physiotherapist after having the children. She agreed and said how much better she felt to be acknowledged in her own right in the hospital instead of 'just being the person who answers the vicarage door'.

The added independence and status which money brings is obviously important but for some the financial aspect is very definitely secondary. Younger couples agreed that the flexibility of the vicar's job made it possible for a wife to pursue her own career more easily. This was endorsed by Cathy, a GP, who said it helped her to know that if she could not be there when the children got in from school, her husband usually could. Sue, a part-time teacher, said, 'Peter has always been keen on taking an active part in the children's growing up and I am convinced that parish life makes this possible. There must be many families where the children only see Daddy at breakfast time or weekends — and then he may be at the golf club.' These acknowledgements of the benefits of vicarage life are very cheering!

In the past, when most clergy had wives based

on home, there was usually somebody with whom to share anxieties during the day, over the lunch table or a cup of tea. Many now find that their wives cannot fulfil this supportive role in the same way or to the same extent. For some this is a new experience in middle age. It can be devastating at first to be the one left alone at home when a wife gets a job. A vicar told me that although he coped well enough, he could never really get used to it and he knew that parishioners did not call so much because they found it strange and empty without his wife.

Many younger clergy expect and accept this situation from the beginning of their married lives. Ian and Barbara told me that at first they had only managed to spend every other Saturday together. She commuted daily during the week, leaving home at 8.00 am, sometimes not returning until 9.00 pm, so that Ian's free time was quite lonely and he tended to continue working instead of giving himself time to relax. Eventually, they reached a compromise and she took on part-time work instead.

Pressures are also caused by the fact that modern couples have much higher expectations of the marriage relationship than most people in previous generations. Wives who are only free in the evenings and at weekends can easily come to resent their husband's constant absence from the house at meetings, services, and weddings and the demands that individual parishioners make on them. Families who have been used to relaxing together at weekends in the years before ordination often find that particular change in their lives very hard. Some dislike parishioners' expectations that they will be personally involved while others bemoan the fact that they can share so little of their husband's work. It seems hard enough to find the right parish for the right person at times so it is an even happier outcome if both find fulfilment of their hoped-for roles in the same place!

Difficulties can arise when a wife has a bigger salary or a higher position in a secular job. A psychotherapist who has clergy couples among those she counsels, referred to 'a payment to set somebody free', intimating that some husbands may find the personal sacrifice involved in agreeing to their wife working is worth it for the sake of her own fulfilment and ultimately the happiness of their marriage. Wives who are not sympathetic to their husbands' calling, either from the start or because they have become embittered by their experience of parish life, often find that they are much happier if they are employed, with some independence of their own.

Clergy husbands

Families where the wife is the ordained partner are almost all likely to have two incomes, as most clergy husbands have their own job. Many will have helped to support their wives financially during their training and have been interested and personally involved throughout. Sadly, some have not bargained in advance for the upheaval that parochial ministry would mean for their lives together and there seems to be a fairly high incidence of marriage breakdown as a result. This is particularly so where a husband has 'only gone along with' his wife's aspirations to be ordained.

Vicky is a woman deacon with two teenagers. She told me that at first everything went well. The family moved with her into a curate's house only a few miles away from their original home parish so the children remained at the same school and her husband's job in a multi-national firm was not affected. However, when he was offered promotion which would mean moving to another part of the country, the clash of interests became too great for them to cope with and eventually they parted by mutual agreement.

A thoughtful husband said, 'You could take the line that my wife's first vocation was marriage — to me — and this is only her second vocation so it should take second place. Husbands who think like that should make it clear right from the beginning because it's almost bound to end in disaster.' I have met many husbands who are very proud and supportive of their wives and take an active role in the life of the parish, also doing their share of the housework and being happy to welcome people into their homes. This seems to be easier for younger couples, who have grown up with the idea of a woman having her own career or vocation and who expect to bring up children as more of a joint exercise than was the case for previous generations.

Women entering the ordained ministry are increasingly doing so at a younger age than previously, so it may well be that their 'first' vocation is ordination and marriage their second, in direct contrast to the example previously quoted. Jemma, a woman deacon who went to theological college straight from university said, 'I knew from about the age of twelve that I wanted to be ordained. There has never been any other life for me.' She married during her training. Her husband has his own business and in spite of some teething troubles at first over practical matters, there has been a steady growth of mutual support during the early years of their marriage. In another case, when the first baby arrived, the wife was able to arrange leave of absence. Many couples said how much they wished there was more possibility of job-sharing.

The clergy couple who are both ordained ministers deserve a whole book of their own! This situation is still relatively new but will become increasingly common. An interesting booklet, *Couples in Ministry*, was produced in 1988 by the Ministry Committee of the diocese of Sheffield. It tells the stories and experience of seven couples in their own words. In his introduction, the Bishop of Sheffield remarks 'there is no pattern in these ministries . . . no blueprint for couples in ministry emerges.' However, it makes helpful reading for others in similar areas of work.

Choosing to stay at home

Audrey, a professional, middle-aged wife, spoke of how she had weighed up her feelings about the change in relationships and atmosphere brought about through the Women's Movement. She felt that wives were under pressure, made more intense by TV advertising, to be superhuman, holding down their jobs, organizing the house and taking part in parish life all at the same time and equally effectively. She regretted the lack of leisure time together that she observed in the lives of many clergy couples. In her own case, she made a conscious decision not to continue with her own career, although she would 'dearly love the stimulus of a full-time job', in order to share her husband's day off and be around more when he was at home.

My own experience of vicarage life was mainly as a 'parish' wife after the first three years, enjoying bringing up our young family and seeing Michael's vocation as a way of life rather than just a 'job'. Although at times I rather resented being taken so much for granted and felt undervalued, I really liked being part of a very active and caring community. In the past this was the norm, but clergy wives who stay at home today (and they are still reasonably plentiful) may find they are among the relatively few women in the parish who are around and therefore available during the day. This can place a real burden on them, since people are apt to think that they have plenty of free time. Other members of the family see them as the natural people to have in-laws to live with them (not least because vicarages are fairly large with a spare room often available).

Some wives in this position told me that they really felt they were the underdogs with no status of their own, in a world where women have learned to demand their rights. Dilys, whose husband is vicar of a suburban parish in the South

West, said how furious she had felt when she asked the churchwarden if his wife would like to help to make new curtains for the parish hall, a job she hated personally but at which the other lady was expert. 'Oh no, she's very busy at the moment', he said. 'But so am I', she replied, only to receive the answer 'Yes but it's your job!' She said it took her breath away. He must have got a blast when he told his wife because he did at least have the grace to apologize at church next Sunday.

A teenage son was very outspoken in defence of his mother, Dolly, telling me that she worked as hard as his father, harder than their parish Reader or any other parishioner. He thought she should be acknowledged more. Clergy wives made to feel guilty by such a paragon of virtue will doubtless say that it is her choice if she wishes to be so involved. In this particular case I can vouchsafe that her concern is completely genuine and has no strings attached. She loves people and is much loved in return. She sees her work in the parish, visiting people, helping to run organizations such as pram groups and working with young mothers (married and unmarried), as a way of using her own talents. Her vicarage is always welcoming and is a real centre for everybody. In return, she knows that there will always be help when she needs it herself. When her daughter got married, she warned her son-in-law that he was 'not just taking on my family but all the rest of the parish as well!'

Some wives may use their educational skills to lead study groups or help with confirmation classes, or assist in a more official manner by training to be Readers. Women like this who find personal fulfilment in the role of traditional vicar's wife may make it difficult for their successors, who may not want to be committed to the parish and their husband's ministry in the same way. I was told in graphic language by a wife in the South East, that she had no troubles, as her predecessor had done a great hatchet job on the role already, and cleared the way for her by refusing to take on anything that had previously been the vicar's wife's 'job'.

Other wives in similar circumstances admitted that they felt themselves to be considerably poorer than most other people, even though they had a house provided, since their families lived on only one income. Sometimes pressure from children, in an increasingly materialistic world, caused them to feel anxious and inadequate. When our family lived in a vicarage, for many years there were few extra sources of income apart from my occasional supply teaching. We usually felt that our comparative lack of this world's goods was no real problem and that we were somehow released from the competition which prevails in modern society. One of my sons, when aged eleven, discovered (from a graph they had done at school) that I was the only mother in his form who had not got an electric mixer! We laughed and agreed that it would only be another thing to clean. As we lived in a fairly prosperous area, we developed a kind of family motto to remind the children of real values. They still repeat it to us, with varying expressions, all these years later: 'It's not what you've got, it's what you ARE.'

We certainly lived on the breadline in the early years. The family laughed incredulously at the story of our journey to hospital, the day before the birth of our eldest son. I travelled the five miles on a bus while my husband kept pace on his moped with my suitcase strapped on behind him; we managed to have a taxi to take the new baby home! More recently, a neighbouring vicar's wife told me that her children seemed to be the only ones in the neighbourhood who did not possess BMX bikes. She found this all the more ironical because in their last parish, in a very deprived area, they had always feared that their family had more than anybody else.

Lack of money was not mentioned as a cause of anxiety by many people, which I found fairly surprising. It was frequently remarked, particularly by people who had grown up in vicarages themselves, that the clergy are much better off than in the past. Expenses are regarded by a generation aware of such things, as fair and normal, though some older clergy still find it embarrassing to ask, if arrangements have not been clearly made prior to their arrival in a parish. This can be a shock, as one middle-aged wife remarked: 'In our last parish we got £3000 a year for expenses. Now we're in a poor inner-city parish and we get £600! I don't know how long we can go on subsidizing it unless I go out to work.' Those who had previously had higher incomes before ordination tended to feel it most. One wife said that as they had 'dropped' £10,000 she doubted if they would manage without her additional income, yet others who had come down even more seemed to manage quite happily on a single clergy stipend.

Clergy couples in the community

There is one definite area in which a clergy family really is different from most others: the expectations which parishioners will have of them. In the ordination service, the man or woman is asked by the bishop, 'Will you strive to fashion your own life AND THAT OF YOUR HOUSEHOLD according to the way of Christ?' The person about to be ordained replies 'By the help of God, I will.' This public commitment assumes that the family also accepts and will be involved in the ministry about to be undertaken.

At this point I am prepared to stick my neck out! Personally I think the most unfortunate thing a wife can say when she moves into a parish is that she is 'not a clergy wife'. No doubt, some will disagree with me. However, first impressions take a long time to dispel. The result of such a remark is likely to be that parishioners may not understand at first, and some never will, what she is actually trying to say, since they see her living in a tied house and married to a clergyman.

The discerning will realize that she is really attempting to make it clear that she does not want to be judged by their preconceptions of what a clergy wife should be like, what she should do and how she should behave. But there are other ways of letting people know that she is an individual in her own right and that she prefers not to be labelled. This also applies to clergy husbands, although parishes seem to expect less of them. As I have already pointed out, men find it easier to pursue their own careers married to a woman deacon, whether they are bus drivers, solicitors or (one I recently heard about) a self-employed watchmaker.

Although couples often moan that they can never feel really off duty in their homes, some still stubbornly resist the advice they would be giving to parishioners with similar problems. Modern technology has blessed us with the answerphone, yet many still complain in exasperation about interrupted meals while refusing to install such a fundamental aid to privacy and occasional peace. Clergy families who do not take regular time off, or try to be together as much as possible, become tired and stale. Holidays are essential and there are generous grants and offers of accommodation available from many sources for those who might not otherwise afford it. Several families told me that buying a caravan was the best thing they ever did.

It is not unusual to meet people who find parochial ministry less harassing than it is often claimed to be. Philip, a curate in his second year, said that his life was much less busy than before he was ordained. In his previous work, as a teacher, there was considerably more stress. He had been constantly and deeply involved in the life of his local church, where he was also a Reader. This meant that as a layman he had often been out at night and given up his free time at weekends. His wife confirmed this and said that she saw much more of him now and remarked on how close the family felt they had become.

Another curate's wife wrote to me, quite forcefully: 'Although I realize that life in the curate's house may well be different from life at the vicarage, so far I find that it is a myth that the phone is constantly ringing and people always calling.' This attitude can often change with experience. One of the times in a clergy marriage when problems seem to loom largest is when the family moves. Each occasion will be a new challenge but by far the biggest jump is from curate to vicar. A young wife found it overwhelming, after 'being rather spoiled when we were in a curate's house, without any ultimate responsibility and feeling close to the parishioners — especially the young ones — suddenly we were in at the deep end.' She found that her husband was out more than when he was a curate, the doorbell and telephone were busier and they both felt much less private. As she remarked, 'Now we really know that the buck stops here!'

Such attitudes are not always understood by older clergy, who grew up in an age when the stiff upper lip and strict discipline predominated. Nor are parishioners necessarily sympathetic. Although most have a 'two-part' day themselves and can decide how they spend their evenings, they do not easily accept that the vicarage family may wish for some time off together during the week. Some younger clergy incline to the theory, sometimes nurtured at college, that they can build their ministry round the family. It has already been pointed out in chapter three that theological colleges try to prepare ordinands for the reality of parish life but, as one curate put it, 'For all I had known many clergy and had lots of talk with them about the job. I had totally under-estimated how much you become parish proper-ty. Everyone wants you, your time, your input.' He was surprised to find how many people fail to realize that you need some time to yourself and some privacy.

One ordinand with five children told me that he did not intend to go to meetings when he was in a parish, as he considered them to be a waste of time. When I remarked that there are normally quite a number he replied. 'Well, we shall just have to educate the parishioners.' I hope he for-gave me when I said 'Good luck'.

The experiences clergy and their partners have at the beginning of their parochial ministry are very important. Curates can take their cue from the vicar and share his enthusiasm, or lack of it, for a disciplined pattern of prayer, a ministry of teaching and pastoral care. They may respond or react to the pattern presented to them. Both hus-band and wife will see (and learn from?) the examples of clergy couples around them. One in-cumbent told me in graphic detail how he was on duty at the crematorium for a whole week, soon after he was ordained deacon. He took thirty-eight funerals. It affected him so badly that he had to go and be sick several times. The same man admitted to having preached at least seventy times during that first year as a curate. His wife said she rarely saw him. A very different picture emerged from an account by a vicar's wife who wrote that they remembered her husband's first curacy seventeen years earlier with great affection. They were blessed with 'an excellent vicar and his wife; this laid the foundation for our work today.'

It used to be said that clergy should not have friends in their parishes, but many, usually younger couples told me that the less formal atmosphere of today makes this much more acceptable. However, it can produce problems so needs to be handled with tact. A thoughtful parishioner commented that it seems odd that clergy preach about love but some of them find it hard to express it in a normal way. He agreed that members of a congregation can be jealous when they see others on apparently 'favoured nation' terms, especially if they have reason to think that confidential matters may be discussed.

Increasingly, in a world where people are apt to speak more openly about themselves than in the past, many members of a church congregation appear to understand that the vicarage family is just as human as they are themselves. When I was a vicar's wife I felt that I could never talk about my family background or share my experiences of the past. That would not be so today. Each person is different, so for some it will be harder to share their humanity, especially what may be considered as signs of weakness or failure. Depression and mid-life crisis are all common to clergy families, as they are to other professions. It can help when parishioners realize this. There is nothing unusual about the priest who finds himself in the pulpit, offering words of wisdom to the faithful, just after a stand-up row with his teenage daughter. Most of his listeners should be able to identify with that!

Diocesan attempts to affirm and support

Some older clergy have remarked to me that they find their younger colleagues much more dependent than their own generation. A bishop said that he was sometimes amazed at the things people telephoned him about, which he would never have considered asking advice on when he was a vicar himself. In his home there is a joke about clergy who are so unsure of themselves that they almost ring up to ask what colour toilet paper they should put in their parish hall. One retired gentleman said, rather unkindly, 'Some of them need nursemaids nowadays.'

Apart from tensions which are caused from actually living in the vicarage, the feeling that some have of being a 'separate breed', a 'race apart' (both phrases used to me by clergy wives) and the problems which may be endemic in the marriage relationship and the family, the modern 'clergyperson' may feel pressures of quite another kind. The very nature of his or her calling makes the 'job' different and, to many people, incomprehensible. Many clergy, particularly those in their middle years, find themselves in a state of uncertainty where once they were very positive and were acknowledged leaders in their communities. They find it hard to explain what they do, in layman's terms, specially to non-believers. In some parts of the country the multi-faith society challenges them face to face.

A wise priest suggested that all clergy should read through the ordination service each year on their anniversary, preferably with their wives if married, to remind themselves of the declaration they made: 'I believe that God has called me.' Many clergy nowadays, of all persuasions, have found it very helpful to have a spiritual director. This does not necessarily have to be a priest (although that would be needed if one wished to make one's confession). Some people find that a woman deacon or lay person is very helpful. The important thing is that they should be able to listen, advise and encourage spiritual growth, with understanding and compassion. This is open to all Christians of course. It seems particularly worth recommending to clergy wives and husbands of ordained women, who should hardly be expected to receive spiritual direction from their partners (who in any case may be the very stumbling blocks about which they are seeking advice).

Bishops have become more aware of the need for individual support, particularly as their own work load makes it difficult for them to give as much time as some feel desirable (see Appendix 2). In the Liverpool diocese, clergy and accredited lay workers have been encouraged since 1978 to take part in a Joint Work Consultation. This is an attempt by somebody already known and trusted to assess and assist the approach to the work-load which is carried. The two bishops also hold themselves accountable to each other for a Work Consultation for half a day once a year. More recently, a three-year Appraisal in Ministry has been introduced which takes place with the area dean. Some wives have told me that the experience gained from these has also helped their husbands to share more openly with them. Many dioceses are engaged in similar exercises.

Various other ways in which clergy may be helped include post-ordination training, intended as a continuation of that done already while in residential colleges or on courses. Some aspects of this may also involve partners and can be very useful (if only because then they can meet each other, air their views and let off steam!). At a later stage, many dioceses offer 'in-service training' to revive flagging spirits and widen horizons.

Clergy are increasingly urged to take a sabbatical leave, if possible every seven years. Grants are available and many find that such a break, lasting up to three months, gives a new lease of life. Some spend a term at a university or in an academic institution abroad (such as Tantur in the Holy Land). Others make a study of an ecumenical project or other particular interest by living alongside another group of people, perhaps in a monastery or a parochial setting completely different from their own.

It is often possible for partners, even whole families, to share this time. Couples who have no family at home and where both are able to be away for a prolonged period together find it a wonderful experience. I have twice gone on sabbatical leave with Michael, each quite different and both very worthwhile. The first was what we called our 'ecumenical crawl', making our way — some of it with a caravan — via Rome and Athens, by land and sea to the Holy Land, meeting Christians of every tradition on the way. The second was an idyllic three months spent at the chaplaincy in Pau, in South-West France. We lived in a flat, spending six hours a day doing academic work, with one day off each week which we usually spent exploring the Pyrenees, only twenty miles away.

Young families speak with real affection of living in country cottages, where father and mother pursue their own study while the children attend the local school for a whole term, leaving time to walk and play together and have weekends where they can sit together in church. Simon, a twelve-year-old from a vicarage in the inner city, told me about his family's experience of just such a sabbatical. He quite took my breath away when he said, 'Yes, it was very interesting . . . being on the other side.'

Mutual support

The isolation experienced by some clergy couples proves impossible to help in certain cases. There is a long tradition in the Church of England of doing your own thing, running your own show. However, it is now very common to have combinations, of teams or groups, legally constituted, where several clergy work in conjunction with one another. Some are Local Ecumenical Projects. This shared ministry means that clergy couples often form close, mutually supportive relationships with each other and can also include single men and women. Married couples in ministry together usually find that working in such circumstances suits them very well. They can both live on the spot but work in different parts of the parish.

Such arrangements vary greatly as to their success, with the inherent weakness that so much depends on the characters and personalities of their clergy. Some people have found the whole experience very uncomfortable. Jake, a team vicar in the North East, told me that he never wanted to work in a team again, after the in-fighting and lack of co-operation which he had felt undermined his own ministry, making his wife very unhappy. But there are many others who have found it very helpful and enjoyed belonging to a 'family' (which is the ideal, after all) with shared values and mutual support.

Some clergy and wives who feel isolated have formed their own informal groupings and support networks, hoping for a similar sharing of experience and friendship. However, this can lead to unexpected difficulties, as Don and Madge illustrated when they described living for twelve years in an inner-city parish. They moved their daughter from their church school when she was seven. She was becoming introverted, as the only child of the vicarage, in a multi-racial group where she was clearly being victimized. In this case, the surrounding clergy were not sympathetic and said that it showed they were not really committed to the area.

Wives vary in their response to special clergy wives events but they usually seem to appreciate locally arranged quiet days or evenings. Each diocese organizes these things in its own way, some going so far as to hold regular clergy wives' day conferences or even residential ones lasting three days. Nearly half the dioceses have produced handbooks for clergy wives during the last few years, usually on the initiative of bishops' wives, as a way of keeping in touch and welcoming new-comers. They include plenty of basic information (including what to do and what help they will be offered if their husbands should die in office).

Some wives find companionship with others in weekly meetings for Bible study. Others just want to chat and relax. There are often local groups, which may or may not be very organized. Jill, the wife of a late ordinand formerly in business, living on the outskirts of a univesity city in the South East, wrote to me: 'Within the church community there is support for me and the clergy wives' group in this area is a very loving, caring and fun group of women.' She went on to ask, 'Where was the Company Wives' Support Group?' Men married to women deacons do not seem as yet to have shown many signs of wishing to be organized. However, Reg, a father of two with a job in administration, did remark that he would quite enjoy sharing some of his experiences with others: for example, how he feels about 'sitting with the kids in the congregation, while Mum takes the service!' He and others suggested names for themselves other than 'clergy husband' or 'clergy spouse', but as yet nobody seems to have arrived at a satisfactory answer.

Spiritual dimension

Ultimately, the clergy should be able, in most situations, to find their main support group from within the parish. In many places, where a person is on their own (the usual pattern after moving from a curacy) it is possible to gather a group who will say the daily offices together and pray for the needs of the community. It is increasingly recognized that praying is not just the job of the vicar.

Encouraging parishioners to go to retreats or quiet days and to acknowledge that the clergy also benefit from and need such experiences, helps to build an understanding of the real nature of their work. One wife wrote to me: 'I think that among the best things is the acceptance by people of the spiritual dimensions of one's life, even if they are not committed to any faith of their own.'

Clergy couples may have found spiritual help through their experience of the charismatic movement, the ministry of healing, or Ignatian spirituality. They may have been analysed by the Myers-Briggs Temperament Sorter and the enneagram. However, I was interested to meet many for whom these had turned out to be 'not the whole picture' and ultimately not very satisfying. It seems to be summed up well by a middle-aged priest who said to me: 'I've tried the lot and in the end I've returned to the pattern that has always worked best for me. I ring my church bell, morning and evening, and my parishioners know that I am tuning in to the great stream of worship offered daily by the church. I am not alone.'

6
Not in
Your Own Strength

WHEN SUPPORT IS NEEDED

'I believe in a God who expects me to stand on my own feet.' This remark by an elder statesman of the church sums up well the attitude which still prevails among many clergy who work autonomously in their own patch.

It shows little regard for the span of care which I shall be attempting to describe in this chapter. It deserves respect as an admirable philosophy to some extent, pointing up the need for personal growth and for taking responsibility for our own lives. However, it does little for the man or woman, married or single, suffering from stress, who genuinely feels the need for outside help, except to burden them with a double load of guilt. Clergy are particularly aware of their public image and there is a natural fear of being 'marked down', especially if their anxieties concern marriage problems.

Lay people have remarked to me that they think some clergy are self-indulgent, even self-pitying on this subject. Many jobs impose stress in varying degrees, some to intolerable levels. Businessmen, teachers and others suggest that it is time clergy stopped worrying about themselves and counted their blessings. They do not have to commute, they have a home provided, job security and plenty of variety. They are not answerable to an office boss, are not held responsible for the failure of a business project or for children's examination results. On the whole they are likely to see much more of their wives and families than most of their parishioners.

However, it is a fact that pastoral care for the clergy has increasingly meant that their problems have to be taken seriously. This has been recognized only gradually during the last twenty years and is at last being addressed on a more professional basis. Some clergy feel very isolated in the responsibility for a parish, since it is a geographical area with thousands of people to whom they are expected to extend care. This very fact will involve them in encounters with total strangers appearing on the doorstep, demanding a suitably polite response to their requests for baptisms, weddings, counselling and various other services. They find themselves dealing with families who never darken the door of the church but who still require comfort when they suffer bereavement.

A fairly high proportion are inclined to perfectionism and tend to be over-scrupulous. This characteristic makes them feel that they can never finish, never really complete their work because there are still so many people round them who remain untouched by the love of God (which after all is what prompted their own initial response). This makes their calling a 'burden' and they suffer from guilt and feelings of inadequacy.

In 1989, I presented a programme on Radio Merseyside in which Michael and a middle-aged vicar talked about the subject of burnout. The vicar spoke honestly and straightforwardly about his own experience. His thoughts were as follows:

I am the vicar of a busy parish in a lovely part of Merseyside. In the eyes of many people it could be said that our church is very successful . . . we have one of the largest congregations in the Liverpool diocese. I am very ably assisted by a team of Lay Readers, the envy of many of my colleagues . . . a host of people give generously of their time and talents. What more could I ask for? Yet a few days after my fiftieth birthday I collapsed whilst taking assembly at our church school.

It was diagnosed by the doctor as a 'stress and exhaustion reaction', in other words burnout. I had burnt the candle at both ends, carrying the worries and burdens of my parish . . . it was as if a fuse had blown, my body let out a warning that enough was enough.

My first reaction, once I had recovered from the initial shock, was that of failure. After working for ten years in this busy and exciting parish I suddenly felt that I could not cope . . . I was of no further use. I had let down so many people, my parish, the new curate who had only just arrived as well as my family. Like most clergy I was a bit of an extrovert . . . nothing pleased me more than to walk through our village, stopping to talk with the many people to whom it was my privilege to minister. Now I could not go out of the front door and when one day I needed to go to the bank, the visit was only accomplished because my daughter took me by the arm and accompanied me there. I was down, out and finished!

My road to recovery began with the love and support of my parish, family and fellow clergy, who with prayers and loving concern supported me in a very wonderful way. But perhaps the first real step in hope came when sharing my fears of failure with my bishop. He reminded me that we preach a gospel of failure, for in the eyes of many people the crucifixion of Jesus was nothing short of failure. After all, had he not come to save the world, only to finish up by hanging upon a cross? As St Paul puts it, 'we preach Christ crucified, a stumbling block to the Jews and foolishness to the Gentiles.' As I look at Jesus upon the cross and hear his cry 'My God, My God, why have you forsaken me', I see in a very, very small way what he must have felt like, despised and rejected . . . a failure.

That, however, was not the end of the story for very soon after came the resurrection and that has been my hope and vision. Gradually, with tremendous support from my wife and members of my church, I reach out to that glorious message of Easter, the message that tells me that what was apparently a failure led on to a new life.

I crashed, I felt a failure, but with God's strength I am coming through.

After this programme, large numbers of people said how much it had helped them to know that it could happen to clergy too and they felt closer to their own vicars as a result. That vicar's wife, who is a nurse, told me that her personal difficulty during this time was losing her own support, since she had always drawn comfort from him. Now he had become 'an empty vessel'. She was greatly helped by their friend, a Roman Catholic priest, with whom their church shared in a local covenant scheme. The teenagers in the family found the length of time needed for a recovery made them very anxious and they constantly asked each other 'Will Dad ever be all right?' This illustrates what is generally recognized: that personal worries can affect working patterns and vice versa, so when one or the other becomes a problem for a clergy family it might be thought to be more complicated since both are so inextricably mixed together in the home.

There can be few jobs where people are subjected to such fragmented days. However well organized, clergy are always open to unexpected emergencies, calls and experiences. On Monday morning the week ahead may appear to be reasonably free but by the afternoon four funerals may have come in, making havoc of the neat arrangements. These also entail visits to the bereaved families, comforting and caring for them in a situation usually full of grief for them but perhaps all too familiar to the priest, who must remain sensitive in each individual situation.

Nancy and Bill spoke to me about their feelings when their own twenty-three-year-old daughter died in a car crash. Parishioners in their poor, town parish tried to comfort them in the only way they knew, as Nancy explained 'by putting their arms round us'. The first funeral Bill had to conduct shortly afterwards was that of a sixteen-year-old boy. Another priest told me about his own difficulties one day when he buried a six-month-old baby, the victim of a cot death, followed almost immediately by conducting the funeral of a man who had committed suicide. In these cases long-term support will also be needed for the families. The question remains however: who cares for the carers?

Counselling

The previous experience of clergy who come from jobs in industry and similar professions has often been that of working in a team, discussing decisions with others who are equally involved, thus not bearing the sole responsibility. In addition, anybody born since the Second World War has grown up in the welfare state and has been used to knowing that in most departments of life there is a safety net. They will not find the idea of talking over their problems as strange as some older clergy who may find it hard to acknowledge them. Others who are apparently extrovert may share this inability because they have kidded themselves that their lives are well organized and they are too proud to acknowledge weakness or failure.

A counsellor for Relate (formerly Marriage Guidance) told me that she found it to be the same in any profession. Many business firms nowadays spend considerable amounts of money on counselling services to assist their employees and feel it is worth their while. It was pointed out that if the RAF spend up to £4 million to train a pilot, they are naturally concerned about his psychological balance. Large firms like ICI and British Telecom also see that workers can receive help.

Local support

Many dioceses have established caring groups or individuals with an 'official' status but operating with complete confidentiality. An example of shared responsibility is to be found in the Inter-Diocesan Counselling Service (IDCS) in the North West, serving the dioceses of Blackburn, Carlisle, Chester, Liverpool and Manchester. A number of counsellors from each are available for clergy and their partners from any part of the area, thus enabling them to go outside their own diocese, which they may find more acceptable.

In reply to my question 'To whom would you go for advice if you really needed it?' I was constantly told that it would not be to the 'hierarchy' (bishops and archdeacons) and not usually to anybody recommended by the diocese, but to friends 'outside'. This seems to be partly due to fear of the lack of confidentiality. Also, as Brian and Joyce said, 'We wouldn't want to think that every time we met the bishop he was thinking of Brian as a "problem".' However, diocesan counsellors obviously are used by some and those who spoke to me were all trained men and women of great integrity. One couple said that they felt there had been a distinct change, when comparing attitudes to vicarage life, around 1970. This was a time they saw as a watershed, as people who grew up during and after the 1960s had a more open, questioning upbringing, especially with regard to the role of women.

It was suggested to me by one counsellor that among those called to ordination there tends to be a preponderance of rather sensitive people, some of whom are loners, a good number being only children. This is borne out by the findings of the Myers-Briggs experiments on temperament types. Many of these are natural 'carers' but are shy and reserved themselves. This type of person may find it easy to appear confident and six feet above contradiction on Sundays but they lack experience of the give and take of family life which would have prepared them for parochial ministry.

Many clergy who seek help appear to have fairly minor problems, which may of course be masking something more serious. Often simply by going to talk things over in a relaxed, informal atmosphere, it seems that men and women of all ages, from twenty to sixty in one counsellor's experience, can be helped considerably. It is very difficult to generalize on these matters, since one person may seek just one visit while another will continue to need help over several months. Obviously, counselling is often thought of mostly in terms of marital problems but in fact there are many other causes of stress.

Tensions which result from difficulties with parishioners can become extreme. Relationships with churchwardens, organists, choir members and not least the prospect of trouble at a Parochial Church Council meeting may bring anxieties out of all proportion to their real importance. So can the pressure involved in keeping confidences which make for deep relationships with individuals. It is not unusual for clergy and others in positions of trust to abuse their positions of intimacy, since spirituality and sexuality are closely connected, (a subject dealt with in *Sex in the Forbidden Zone*, by Peter Rutter). All too often, these particular problems are not addressed in time and then escalate into clerical scandals, open to revelation in the gutter press.

Simply coping with the role versus the reality in a parochial situation can prove to be a much greater strain than many imagine. This was described to me in some detail by a married couple, both in the ordained ministry, who worked in separate parishes. They tended to spend their leisure time together in discussing their various parochial problems. Yvonne said that they finally went for advice to another clergy couple who both worked as counsellors. Talking things over with them helped them to realize just how much they were both living the job in a rather self-conscious way to the exclusion of any other interests. A situation which a counsellor suggested might become more of a problem in the future was where a 'traditional' vicar's wife might feel threatened by a curate's wife who is ordained herself, giving her status as a trained minister, whether she is attached to that parish or elsewhere. I found it interesting that there seems to be relatively little difficulty over single women working in parishes.

Stress factors

Other problems arise from the general feeling that many clergy have that they are seldom praised or have their work affirmed, since lay people do not see the need. 'I just get sick of seeing Christine being taken for granted,' said John, a hard-working vicar in a market town in the South West, whose wife is tireless and perhaps over-involved in parish affairs. The answer to this kind of grouse may be to move to another area, giving a fresh start and a different situation.

In some cases, people are promoted 'above their ceiling' and it can be hard to come to terms with one's own inadequacy. One priest told me that he tried hard to see his failures and hurts as 'sharing Christ's wounds', since suffering must surely be an integral part of our Christian experience. Some cannot cope alone with this and may need to be reassured that times of darkness, depression, sometimes rebellion, are not abnormal.

Many of the stresses concerned with marital and family problems are shared equally with lay couples. These include the issue of authority and headship in the marriage partnership, brought into sharp relief today and running counter to feminist theories. But in addition, clergy wives who work outside the home may find themselves mixing in a very secular world where people may not share their ideals and values at all. This can make them less sympathetic to the apparent 'churchiness' of their husband's more confined relationships.

Allied to the problems of job sharing, the pressures on children can be very great, as they become the meat in the sandwich while their parents attempt to work out new patterns of work and care. This particular problem is both easier and harder in clergy households because working hours are undefined, although flexible, unlike the regular hours in most other jobs. There are no clear boundaries due to the 'availability' factor which necessitates being at least reasonably accessible most of the time. In addition, as one counsellor said, 'In some households there is a constant tug of war between the insistent gospel imperatives concerning wealth and status-conscious modern society, where televisions and washing machines are taken for granted, micro-wave ovens and video recorders are unremarkable and many households possess at least one word processor.'

Serious cases will be passed on, if necessary, to other professional psychotherapists. However, clergy couples who need help may find some methods of counselling unacceptable as they vary considerably and some are based on very secular assumptions. There is a growing awareness that if therapeutic advice starts on this basis Christians may find themselves at odds with biblical assumptions and in conflict with society. This can prove to be very difficult for clergy couples who may find it unacceptable, so will not be helped. An example quoted on this aspect was that of sex, where the secular view may be that one satisfies oneself or refuses one's partner, to suit oneself, while a Christian view would suggest that the other person should come first.

Marriage breakdown

It is not surprising, in a country where divorce has become so comparatively common, that marriage breakdown should also be found to some degree among clergy couples. The expectations of parishioners or the pressures on a working wife by those who imply that she should be there at her husband's shoulder all the time, may produce additional stress. However, the reasons given for separation or divorce are much the same as for any other couple: they include personal or sexual incompatibility, unfaithfulness or simply growing apart due to work patterns or other matters. I have always considered it unfair, in most cases, to blame the job, since it is often quite obvious that a couple might not have been able to sustain a married relationship whatever the situation.

Nevertheless, clergy have a higher profile locally than most other couples. There is more pressure on them to stay together, when you compare their personal life with that of other people, for instance a probation officer or a secretary, where there is not the same sense of letting the side down. There is a responsibility to parishioners to uphold the state of marriage. One heartbroken lay woman told me that 'Of course we understand that they were genuinely driven to it, conscience-stricken and guilty, but we all feel scarred and rather frightened . . . it has added to our own insecurities to realize that even a clergy marriage may not last.'

In 1983, a survey was undertaken on behalf of the Archbishop of Canterbury, resulting from a motion passed by the General Synod, to establish the number of cases of the breakdown of clergy marriages and the pastoral and practical support provided by or through the church. This resulted, among other things, in annual monitoring of the situation by diocesan bishops. It is now anticipated that there are something in the region of forty to fifty breakdowns a year. Once it was realized that there was a real problem when clergy marriages broke down, steps were taken to alleviate immediate distress and since that time the situation has improved considerably.

It has become clear that each case is unique and every couple sees it differently so the Church finds it is impossible to have set rules. Some couples resist help of any kind, while others have quite unrealistic expectations that all their problems can be solved for them.

Whatever the reason, whoever is 'responsible', in many situations the husband is able to continue in his work or move to another post. This may be particularly traumatic for the wife, who has no right to half the tied house where they have lived together, so she will lose her home as well as her husband and there are likely to be financial problems in addition. Indeed, wives are also likely to suffer not only physically but even more psychological stress may be laid upon them since some may judge that they are somehow the 'guilty party' or that they have not been 'sufficiently supportive'. This has been the experience of many wives in such circumstances and means that they also lose the whole network of the local community of which they have been near the centre.

Each diocese now has a Visitor, officially appointed by the bishop, whose job is to be a facilitator 'to offer pastoral care and practical assistance'. These Visitors meet together once each year to pool information and advice. Some dioceses have established teams with experts who will assist in such matters as housing and social security and also give spiritual help. It is clear that there are more cases of marital breakdown in the South than in the North. It was suggested to me by one Visitor that northern clergy tend to be more indigenous, less prone to move away from their roots and therefore nearer to their wider family networks, thus enabling them to receive more support. This may be so.

The majority of breakdowns occur in the forty-plus age group, at a very vulnerable time of life. Elsie, who had nowhere to go with her two teenage sons after she and her husband decided that life together was intolerable, remarked bitterly that she could hardly go back to mother at her age. The Church Commissioners have been particularly helpful in this sad situation, assisting dioceses to provide housing for wives and families. Of course the dioceses make discretionary grants available and are very aware of their responsibilities in these matters.

Hazel, an ex-wife whose husband carried on an affair for three years, which she endured without confiding in anybody until he finally said he wanted a divorce, told me that her bishop and his wife were 'absolutely marvellous' and helped her to move out into a flat which belonged to the diocese. The parishioners were also very supportive and loving towards her and her daughters. In her case, she said that at the time she had 'a dog, some furniture, £90 in the bank and an ancient car'. Another family, a wife and four children, whose father moved in with a woman in his parish, were looked after and provided with a house by local church people.

Some of those whose marriages broke down years ago and who often found themselves living in 'almost unbearable conditions of poverty', to quote one of them, have now also received help. However, the bitterness with which some regard the Church, having felt that they had been let down at the time of their original distress, still makes it difficult to know how to approach them. One deserted wife lives in a council house and although fully qualified with a degree in chemistry, works as a cleaner.

Perhaps I should say that of all the aspects of clergy marriage which I researched for this book, this is the one which caused me most personal pain and sadness. When it was pointed out to me that the Church of England Pensions Board was no more liable and not legally able to support the partners of broken marriages than a bank, shop or office would be in the same circumstances, I felt unjustifiably shaken.

Broken Rites

A knight in shining armour, in the person of

Frank Field MP, came to the help of deserted and divorced wives, when he helped some of them to form a group known as 'Broken Rites' in 1983, after inviting anyone in this position to a meeting in London at which twenty-three people were present. By 1990 there were 190 members although the secretary thought that there must be at least as many again who were in a similar position. She receives about twenty-five to thirty enquiries a year.

Frank Field is a great campaigner, particularly in the area of pension rights. Like all victims of divorce, clergy ex-wives are not eligible for these or for widows' pensions. Broken Rites hopes to get this changed, not to impoverish the husband (or his second wife, if he has one) but to provide some fair treatment for the divorced wife. It is considered that perhaps there should be a private pension scheme on their behalf. They have managed to persuade various charities to help them with holiday grants and outings for children. Charities like the Sons of the Clergy and others have changed their rules so they can now help children who are living with a divorced mother, if she has not remarried.

It was really pressure from this group which originally persuaded the General Synod to take the action already referred to and of which it approves thoroughly. A mother of nine, after months of despair, found members of Broken Rites were the people who eventually helped her to come to terms with her situation. She said, 'I could shout and scream at them, they were the only ones who really understood.' They have set up their own network of Local Links, in parallel with the officially appointed diocesan Visitors, realizing the value of somebody who can genuinely say 'Yes, I do know how you feel . . . I've trodden the same path myself.' There is no doubt that they fulfil a much needed role in their offer of practical and emotional support.

Bereavement

'On Tuesday I was doing everything . . . on Wednesday it had all gone.' That is how Emma, a clergy widow, described her experience of losing her husband suddenly when he had a heart attack and died in her arms. When the retired clergyman whose job at that time was to assist widows in her diocese came to see her, he told her that she had three alternatives: to buy a house, to rent one or to 'go into a home'. She had very little money, so the first was impossible. He announced that there were no houses available to rent. She was astounded at the third suggestion, considering that she was only in her fifties.

Looking back, thirteen years later, she told me that her first reaction to her husband's death had been to go away somewhere quite different. However, on reflection, she realized that she needed friends and should stay somewhere in the neighbourhood, though not in the parish where they had both ministered. She had always had an independent mind, had never made particular friends in the parish but had plenty of interests outside, although she had been a caring and hospitable wife. She and her husband were much loved both by their parish and the local community.

Always, in those first months of widowhood, at the back of her mind there was the thought that she must find somewhere else to live, so that the diocese could appoint a successor to the living. The day it really struck her that she was no longer 'the vicar's wife' was when she looked out of the vicarage window and saw a funeral entering the church and realized that she did not know who it was that had died. She described the attitudes of the parishioners during the six months she remained in the vicarage as 'very kind . . . I tended either to be ignored or smothered.' Eventually she found a suitable house bought by the Church of England Pensions Board, which she now rents from them. Her initial experience, however unfortunate, was alleviated with speed when the diocesan bishop came to hear of it.

The most appalling story told to me by a widow comes from the 1960s. Norah's husband died of a stroke when he was fifty-one, leaving her to provide for two student children and both grandmothers, who lived with them. When she telephoned her local bishop to say what had happened he said, among other things, that he hoped she realized that she would have to be 'out of the vicarage in a month.'

This was a woman who had married during the war, and lived in part of a tenement building in a northern industrial city constantly subjected to bombing, while her husband was a curate. She spoke of how they suffered the privations of living in constant fear of debt, usually in very poor parishes, so that when her husband died there was virtually nothing in the bank. The panic and in-security of having to find somewhere for five adults to live in a short time was finally reduced by the kindness and generosity of parishioners and a grant from the diocese. Norah found a house which she was able to buy, sharing the cost and ownership with a friend who was also wishing to move home.

This situation naturally arises every time a clergyman dies in office. It is particularly acute when this happens suddenly and unexpectedly. In the same week I visited two recently widowed friends of mine. Both were teachers. One had been married to a businessman, the other to a clergyman. The first had decided to stay, at any rate for the time being, in the home which she and her husband had bought and planned to-gether. She did not want to make any decisions in a hurry. The clergy widow, on the other hand, did not have this choice. This real life example highlights the problem with which clergy fam-ilies are faced. Those who are bereaved lose not only their loved one but their home with all its memories as well.

Margaret lost her husband when she was only forty-one. The local 'squire' offered her a cottage to rent in the village, which she accepted, think-ing that staying in the familiar place would help her three young children to adjust to the new situation. However, this did not work out as she had expected, since they were constantly aware that they no longer lived in the vicarage and were reminded every day of the change in their circum-stances and the absence of their father. Eventually the family moved to a house further away, helped by the Pensions Board.

Some of the examples I have quoted may seem particularly hard but they were by no means unusual in the past. There has been a vast improvement in both the financial help provided and the attempt to ensure personal support for widows in recent years. In addition to help with housing, the Pensions Board is also able to provide a lump sum to undergird future needs (this was £29,700 in 1991). All dioceses now have Widows Officers, who are responsible for assisting families to cope with the complexities which arise in the circumstances, usually in conjunction with the archdeacon. There is much more understanding that time is needed to make responsible decisions about where to live and what will be possible financially, especially if a wife has no independent career.

A case which illustrates the change in awareness of the needs of bereaved families is that of a young widow, whose husband died after a very long illness. They were able to discuss what she and their four children, aged from three to sixteen, should do after he had died, both with each other and with diocesan advisers. In the event, having been wonderfully supported by members of the parish, the family remained in the vicarage for almost a year before moving to a new home not too far away. This might seem to be erring too much on the compassionate side, but it shows how a caring community and diocese can reach out when it is deemed necessary.

The problems referred to in this chapter, indeed

all the subjects covered in this book, are by no means peculiar to the Church of England. They are shared by all Christian ministries and it is clear that equal compassion and concern is expressed by others in very practical ways. This applies particularly to the subject which follows.

Retirement

There is a story about a certain bishop in the earlier years of this century who attempted, while visiting an extremely elderly incumbent, to suggest in a gentle manner that he might be considering retirement. The aged gentleman drew himself up to his full height and, looking him straight in the eye, replied: 'My Lord, when I was appointed here by your predecessor but three, there was no indication that the post was temporary.'

My husband was only the ninth vicar since 1799 when he went to Altrincham Parish Church in 1963. Long incumbencies were the rule in the past and most clergy died in office, usually at a great age. Retirement was impossible for many, as they had neither a home of their own nor the money to acquire one. If a clergyman really needed to retire through old age or disablement, it was only possible to do so (after the Incumbents' Resignation Act 1871) by taking money from the revenues of the Parish he was vacating. This meant that a vicar could find himself losing up to a third of his stipend to the previous incumbent!

The Clergy Retirement Measure came into force in 1976, changing the pattern of ministry considerably. Clergy are no longer allowed to hold a beneficed office (for example as a vicar, archdeacon, residentiary canon or bishop) after the age of seventy. They can retire earlier, from the age of sixty-five, as long as they have completed thirty-seven years' service, or special arrangements can be made for sickness or disablement. This is quite different from conditions in former days. I remember Edward, a very old priest who was my school chaplain during the war. He limped badly and was nearly blind but he soldiered on somehow. I think we were not very kind to him and often laughed when he made mistakes. He was a classicist and must have thought us a bunch of Philistines. A teacher told me that he had been wounded in the First World War and had nowhere to go now that he was old. It makes me ashamed in retrospect.

The Church of England Pensions Board has been mentioned already in this chapter. It produces excellent information booklets of its own but I believe it should be given due credit here, mainly because I have heard unremitting praise from all quarters while preparing to write this book, particularly from widows and retired clergy.

The Board now gives considerable help to those who are retiring. In addition to a pension equal to two-thirds of their final salary, they also receive a lump sum (£19,800 in April 1991). A quarter of all clergy pensioners are assisted with housing, either by renting or through an Equity Sharing Mortgage scheme. If they or their widows are unable to manage on their own, there are a number of residential homes, including those at Lytham,

Scarborough and Worthing. The widowed father of one of my friends enjoys his own bed-sitter at Hindhead, where he plays the organ and has plenty of congenial companionship with like-minded friends.

As many as 400 clergy may retire in one year alone. In 1989, the average age at which clergy left full-time work was 66.6 and many of these appear to be enjoying themselves greatly. This seems to be due partly to the care which is now being taken to prepare for such a big change, a practice already popular in the secular world. Many dioceses hold pre-retirement courses, at which advice is given on various matters, including the necessity to have interests and hobbies, the facilities available for leisure activities and even the apparently obvious business of buying a house.

Noel and Grace, who had been retired for five years when they talked to me, said they wished they had attended such a course, as the first year after they left their parish had been 'frightfully unhappy'. They had not realized how much they would miss living in the vicarage and all the activities attached to being at the centre of parochial life. Grace particularly missed the companionship of the members of the Mothers' Union, in which she had been very involved. Some people do suffer badly from what might be called loss of status, finding it hard to be ordinary parishioners with no inside knowledge. However, others told me that they really enjoyed being able to sit together in church, without the responsibility of office and being free to be more private people. Unlike most other jobs, clergy are usually able to continue working in retirement if they wish. Some actually take on responsibility for a small parish, others do Sunday duty during inter-regnums while parishes are waiting for a new vicar.

'We've never been so well off in our lives . . . the Pensions Board has been most helpful and considerate,' I was told by Lionel, whose home is now a three-bedroomed semi, in a quiet tree-lined cul de sac in Shropshire. He and his wife Greta were helped to buy it with an Equity Sharing Mortgage. Their vicarage was large and roomy but they do not miss the heating bills or the busy doorbell. They chose the house for its size, its manageable garden and because it was near shops and public transport, in case they ever found themselves unable to drive. They are regular wor-shippers at their parish church, where Lionel helps out and also does some pastoral visiting for the vicar, which he loves.

Some of our own happiest experiences of the last few years have been when meeting retired clergy, their wives and clergy widows, out shop-ping, at diocesan events in Liverpool and — best of all — at their annual Eucharist in the cathedral followed by lunch. This is always a very special occasion for the sheer pleasure they show at seeing one another again. Retirement is no longer dreaded, thought impossible or considered as a state of perpetual penury. They certainly give us hope for the future!

It could hardly be suggested that the church looks after the clergy in every aspect of their lives, from the moment they are recommended for training to the grave. No doubt there are some who feel themselves let down or deserted for various reasons. These tend to be the ones we hear about in the media. This, in case anybody should need reminding, is why I set out to write this book!

Nevertheless, it is open to question whether any other organization is quite so aware of the need for support at so many different levels: during training, parochial ministry and in retirement. 'How these Christians love one another!' There are plenty of times when that is said with sarcasm or in sadness. I believe that it can truly be said today in acknowledgement of the church's present attempts to offer help and encouragement to its ordained ministers and their partners.

7
Postscript

BISHOPS AND THEIR WIVES
ARE HUMAN TOO!

I was halfway up the stairs, on my way to take my
rollers out, when the front door of our vicarage
opened and in walked the bishop. Michael was
over at church and the children were playing in
the sitting room. My hesitation was brief: there
was no alternative, so I descended with what I
hoped was a welcoming, confident smile, praying
that he would somehow not notice the strange
shape of my hair beneath its garish scarf.

When Michael walked in, minutes later, he
found the bishop sitting on the settee with all
three children. He had an arm round each of the
boys and our eight-year-old daughter, comfortable
and secure on his knee, was telling him con-
fidentially that she was going to be the first lady
bishop! My own headgear received a somewhat
searing look of disbelief after which I slunk out of
the room to repair the damage and we all proceeded to church for the confirmation.

That was a long time ago. The bishop concerned was Victor Whitsey. He was a friendly,
volatile man who related immediately to people,
especially children. His predecessor as Bishop of
Chester, Gerald Ellison, was his complete opposite in every way since he had a shy nature

which tended to be interpreted by others as stand-offish. Had he been the bishop who caught me in my rollers, neither he nor I would have known how to handle the situation. I think I would probably have bolted.

A few years earlier, Bishop Ellison had asked if he could have a bath at our house before preaching at our patronal festival, as he would be coming straight on from playing in a clergy golf match. I washed the tiled walls of the bathroom in preparation for this great event and made one of the children's rooms available, having first cleared out all their toys. While the bishop had his bath, I fed his chauffeur in the kitchen and sighed with relief when he was finally sitting down at our dining table, pink and squeaky clean. When Michael was made an honorary canon of Chester cathedral a year later, one of our parishioners drew a cartoon showing the bishop peeping over the side of the bath with his mitre on a stool beside him. Underneath was written 'The Bishop had a bath so he made HIM a canon!'

Both these bishops had wives, as different from each other as were their husbands. Jane Ellison was a highly competent, attractive woman who was an excellent hostess with a fairly high public profile. Jean Whitsey was a homely person, who saw her role mostly in the context of the family. They were both very caring supportive wives, doing their best to make Bishop's House into a home as well as a 'public' house. I like to think that we learned from both these couples when we found ourselves in a similar position in later years.

Bishops and their wives do not fall off a cloud or walk out of an egg, fully fledged. They are as human as anybody else, with individual personalities and approaches to their work. Many couples find the transition a difficult experience. Wives are usually regarded as secondary (complementary if they are fortunate) in a much more definite way than other clergy wives. It can be more difficult where children are still young because many of the things I have emphasized in this book as essential to clergy family life are changed irrevocably when the father is made a bishop.

The episcopal office may obscure bishops' personalities from the public eye but in fact they come in all shapes and sizes, from very different backgrounds and traditions. Many were educated at Oxford or Cambridge. Some are 'professional' theologians, coming from a teaching post in a university or theological college, while others have been parish priests during their whole ministry like my husband. They include within their ranks not only a number of monks but also a former banker. Wives are probably even more various, since they simply happen to be women whose husbands have become bishops and that may be all they have in common.

Now that the boot is on the other foot, we try never to forget our own experience of bishops and their wives when we go to parishes or when people come to our home either for serious or social reasons. We were amused but not surprised when other episcopal friends told us they had been amazed to discover that a vicar's wife had actually bought new sheets when they went to stay. I should have done exactly the same in the past! However regrettable, we know that some people, clergy and lay, will have certain perceptions about us in advance. We shall be labelled, expected to behave and think in a particular way, because the purple shirt does seem to be a uniform which hides the man beneath more thoroughly than most.

Coping with change

Friends have told me how they reacted to the invitation to the husband to become a bishop. One couple 'jumped up and down on the bed with excitement' until they suddenly took in what the letter they had just opened was really saying. Others have spoken of being 'completely overwhelmed', feeling 'utterly unworthy, needing to be reassured by close friends'. The present Archbishop of Canterbury, George Carey, is reported to have met his wife in a pub for lunch with the news that he (then Bishop of Bath and Wells) had been asked to accept the highest episcopal office in the land. They agreed that they must pray about it. He suggested that they should go to the cathedral but she said 'What's wrong with here?' so they prayed in the pub garden.

I remember very clearly the day Michael showed me the first letter asking him to consider becoming the Suffragan Bishop of Warrington. I was taken completely by surprise. I did not even know that Warrington was in the Liverpool diocese, or that it was vacant. I went out to the kitchen and made coffee and cried my eyes out. My horizons at that time were almost entirely bounded by my family and our life within the extended community of our parish. I realized only too clearly how such a change would affect us all, particularly the children, then aged fifteen, thirteen and eleven.

In the event my fears proved to be correct. The children were really quite unhappy and missed the familiarity of vicarage life, the predictable tempo of the parochial scene with the church across the lawn and the security of 'belonging' without actually having to think about it. Most of all, perhaps, they missed having Dad around at meal times, not much appreciating or understanding his new role since it meant that he was physically absent for hours at a time, often miles away.

We decided from the beginning that it would not be practical to go round as a family with Michael, as he could be officiating in three different churches on a Sunday. On one occasion we did try taking the children to a confirmation, but the remarks (some of them unrepeatable) in the car on the way home about the 'bunfight' in the parish hall and the loneliness of not knowing anybody, convinced us that it was not a good idea. An eventual compromise was reached. They came occasionally to important services at the cathedral such as ordinations, but on most ordinary Sundays they went with me to a local church where there was a Parish Communion service, the kind of worship to which they were accustomed.

Years later the boys told us how they used to be taunted in the vestry with comments like 'Just because you're the bishop's sons you needn't think you can tell us what to do.' It must be quite difficult for a congregation to absorb a bishop's family without being just a bit self-conscious about it. I remember giving a lift to a girl after church and hearing her say to my own young daughter: 'It must be nice to have a father who's a bishop and to live in that big house.' I knew that the recipient of that rather snide remark was struggling not to say that her bedroom was freezing, that she would much rather be back in our vicarage and that she was missing her old friends dreadfully.

The two teenage daughters of another bishop told me about their experiences. The younger one was eight when they moved. She is a very confident girl who makes friends easily, so she soon settled into the life of the church in the village where they live and has continued to take an active part in everything. However her elder sister, a sensitive, more vulnerable girl, was upset at leaving the lively parish where her father had been the vicar. She missed 'being one of the vicarage children, with people popping in and out'. She felt that she was seen by the vicar's family as 'somehow being in competition' and while their children were frequently on show and involved in church activities, she was never asked to do anything, with the result that she was eventually frozen out.

On a personal note, I shall always be grateful to the parishioners at the church where I worshipped with my children and where I still feel I belong and can be accepted without a fuss.

Another wife told me that she had found her local church to be a 'life-saver' for herself and her children. Each bishop's family works out their own pattern. Stories abound, whether apocryphal or true, about wives who stayed outside in the car reading a book during confirmations. One preferred to sit at the back of the church so that she could gesticulate to her husband if he could not be heard. Another is reported to have produced a magazine, saying to her neighbour, a very proper vicar's wife, 'You must excuse me but he only has three sermons and I know them all by heart'!

One of the problems which confront bishops is the fact that they lose the pattern of spirituality and worship, particularly the saying of morning and evening prayer, which they have previously shared with their parishioners, cathedral chapter or college staff. This was something we had not really thought about in advance. Most bishops' houses have a chapel. Ours is very small, seating only six - a converted coal cellar (a fact which Michael often announces with relish, so people are usually surprised to find how lovely it is!). It has become more and more important over the years and gives us an intimate retreat for the daily offices, our prayers and quiet time, a real need in our rather fragmented lives.

Pubs, palaces and prisons

There is certainly plenty of variety from day to day. I was once told that bishops should be found in pubs, palaces and prisons. In theory this feat, though rather unlikely, is perfectly possible to achieve in a single day. Lunch in the pub with a group of industrial chaplains might be preceded by a confirmation in the local jail and be followed by a garden party at Buckingham Palace. Wherever he goes, a bishop is expected to appear ready and perfectly groomed for his next appointment, even if he has driven fifty miles to get there and it may be the eighth engagement in his day. Virtually nobody, apart from his wife and his secretary, sees the extent of his commitments. These will include the preparation of sermons, endless time spent over appointments to livings, numerous interviews and visits (not least the time given to clergy — and sometimes their wives — who may be in distress) and the expectations which both parishioners and others have of him.

A group of bishops in the northern province told me that they averaged 30,000 miles a year, travelling round their dioceses. This reminded me of a TV programme fifteen years ago about the Bishop of Exeter (then Eric Mercer). He said that the one person he could not do without was his driver, since some of his journeys took two hours each way and he often had to leave home at 5.30 pm, not getting back much before midnight. Our children watched this with some friends shortly before their father's consecration and were quite upset to discover the general animosity towards bishops and the lack of understanding about such aspects of their lives. Michael was once actually quizzed by police when he was parked in a country lane, eating sandwiches and preparing for his next engagement. They, like many others including some clergy, perhaps supposed that bishops always dined sumptuously off silver plate.

Bishops' wives

If the picture of bishops tends to be distorted, that of their wives seems to be even more so. One of them described people's attitudes towards her thus: 'I find that I am either lionized, ignored or resented when I go with him. Sometimes people make it very clear that they want to talk to my husband, not me, while at others they are creeping . . . hoping I may drop a word in his ear on the way home!' Another told me that she actually hated sending word in advance when she went to the induction of a new vicar into a parish. 'It sounds as though I think I'm important but if I don't let them know they go into a tizzy and don't know what to do with me. I don't care where I sit but I hate to embarrass them.' I know exactly what she meant, as I have vivid memories of red-faced churchwardens before the induction of their new vicar, seating plans in hand, saying: 'Oh dear, I don't know where I'm going to put you.' I could almost weep for my more shy sisters in this job, since I am reasonably confident by nature. Yet none of us is very thick-skinned really and I once found it hard to cope when I was moved, rather publicly, into four different seats before the beginning of a service!

I remember hearing a bishop's wife say that she felt redundant after being so useful in a parish. However, most of us realize that we have a very necessary supportive ministry in relation to our husband's needs. Some wives drive their husbands to evening engagements, to give them a rest and share some time together. A small number work officially as their secretaries. One bishop told me with an enormous grin 'Yes, I share my bed with my secretary!' His wife said that she thought 'the opportunities are enormous and I think it is a great privilege.' However, other wives, me included, tend to think it might be a cause of difficulty to some clergy when it comes to very confidential matters. Naturally all of us are fairly constantly involved in answering the phone and the door, making coffee and generally welcoming all and sundry who arrive for numerous meetings and occasions.

People are often surprised to find that a bishop's wife may have a paid job but a good number are professional women today and see themselves as no different from any other working clergy wives and some manage to work part- or full-time. I personally enjoyed teaching fifth- and sixth formers in an independent school in Toxteth (a paradox if ever there was one) one day a week for three years after we moved. It was the only area of my life at that time where I felt valued for myself and I welcomed it. Later, my occasional work on local radio led to programmes on national network, mostly with Derek Jameson — an experience in itself!

Some of us work in voluntary capacities in such agencies as the Citizens' Advice Bureau. Others, including me, are magistrates. One friend said, 'Well, you certainly come across people you wouldn't meet otherwise!' That is definitely true on the Liverpool City bench, of the magistrates, the court officials and the defendants. It is a very secular world with which we need to remain familiar and it helps us to keep our husbands in touch with a world where Christian values are not necessarily taken for granted. Others also become involved in diocesan organizations such as the Mothers' Union. This is something which I have found gives me a wonderful opportunity to get to know the women of the diocese and to work with them for a cause which becomes more vital every day: family life.

There is no doubt that most bishops and their wives see the care and support of the clergy as a very important part of their work. One wife told me that on leaving their city parish they were thanked 'for being dotty about each other, because it shows that marriage can work'. She said that her main concern, after supporting her husband and family, is for clergy wives. She is a tireless, loving woman, whose Christian commitment shines through everything she does. In contrast to her attitudes, I was told by others that 'clergy wives should not have expectations of bishops' wives.' One bishop said he thought that although we lose out personally from our lack of consistent contact with one parish, we are valuable because we come to be recognized as we go about the diocese, 'almost like the last vicar, so we give people security because we're familiar.'

After parish life, where we saw people very regularly in the normal course of events, I found the geographical area of a diocese made consistent relationships hard to sustain in a satisfactory way. It can happen that you become close to somebody in need for a time but then may not see them for months. In the Liverpool diocese, we are really very informal compared with some, with Christian names used habitually (in my case, I am known pretty well universally by my nickname, Steve) but there are times when we feel great regret that we are not able to enter into other people's situations with more depth.

All bishops and their wives find themselves catering for lunches, dinners, or buffets for varying numbers of guests. This was one of the things I personally found very hard when we first moved out of our parish. In the past, there was always plenty of help and usually we were all doing it together for a parish occasion. At first, I simply did not know where to ask for help. However kind local parishioners may be, they rarely understand the way a diocese works. Diocesan bishops have a small permanent staff who undergird them, although that in itself may need handling with some sensitivity. Most of us manage to work out a satisfactory method, using caterers for really big occasions like garden parties for clergy families or a Christmas party for the staff of Diocesan Church House (my own biggest event, feeding around eighty people in the house). There is always a good deal of preparation in addition. It is not unusual for Michael and me to be washing up at midnight after entertaining twenty-five people, then we say 'They probably think we keep a staff of goblins in the kitchen!' All the same, we love having people here, both because we enjoy them for their own sake and want them to have a change (especially the clergy) and because we want to share this beautiful house with as many people as possible.

House or home: family isolation

Contrary to popular myth, most bishops do not live in palaces. However, some do. No doubt it would cause great sadness if bishops refused to live in such traditional homes as Rose Castle, the seat of the Bishop of Carlisle or The Palace at Wells. However romantic these places may sound, they are often quite hard to live in and also usually have some historic rooms open to the public. Bishop's House, Bishop's Lodge, Bishop's Croft are all familiar names and naturally they label their occupants so far as the neighbours are concerned. We always count ourselves rather lucky that our house is called 'Martinsfield', which gives us a certain anonymity when we take shoes to the menders or our clothes to the cleaners! Some bishops live in a cathedral close where their families may enjoy the proximity of the mixed but largely ecclesiastical inhabitants around them. However, a friend in that situation remarked crossly, 'Every time I go out of the front door somebody sees me. They know who comes to dinner, what I'm wearing, see my shopping. . . . Oh, for some privacy!'

Privacy was certainly something which descended on our family when Michael became a bishop, to an extent which we found extraordinary after vicarage life. In this we shared the experience of clergy who have non-parochial jobs and of most parishioners, who have to make friends, be accepted into a new congregation and put down their own roots. Parochial clergy find a ready-made community, however difficult that may be in some cases. A diocese does not have the same kind of identity as a parish, since its boundaries are enormous and it has hundreds of churches, parishes and clergy.

My first task was to try to make the house, a very fine example of 1930s architecture with black and white gables, elegant wooden panelling and floors, beautifully spacious reception rooms, six bedrooms, two bathrooms, four lavatories and a wonderful garden, into a real home for our family. It was soon clear that most of our neighbours, while not unfriendly, tended to live their own rather private lives. I had never known what it was to be physically lonely in my life before but those first few months left an indelible memory of long, cold winter days with unhappy children coming in from school (the boys after a two-hour journey) pronouncing themselves 'Fed up . . . Dad's never here.' They were embarrassed by the image of the house and disliked the fact that it was 'either empty or full of strangers'. They brought very few people home in case it was discovered that their father was a bishop. My own feeling of isolation was greater because I stayed with them rather than going round getting to know the diocese with him.

Our eldest son went off to Kashmir for a year when he was seventeen as a volunteer teacher, but few people really knew him so there were not many enquiries about how he was getting on.

Later, when our daughter went to America on a year's student exchange, followed within a month by the departure of our second son for an equally long absence abroad, it struck us yet again how we had been spoiled in a parish by the interest there had always been in our children and the care and love we had received in times of stress.

The time when I was most personally affected by this set apartness was after I had a serious accident in 1985, breaking one of the vertebrae in my spine, arriving home from France in an ambulance. If we had still lived in a vicarage we should have been inundated by help and kindness of a loving, yet practical nature (apple pies perhaps). As it was, cards, letters and flowers came flooding in from people in the diocese but few actually called. I think that is the 'goblins in the kitchen' syndrome again! Michael was a tower of strength for weeks but I grieved that he received so little support himself. Perhaps we both wore our public faces too brightly!

A bishop's wife who lives in a very rural diocese and whose house is rather remote told me that she had been ill when her husband was away. She was on her own in the house for three days and nights with a temperature of 101°. She said: 'I don't think the neighbours know how to cope with a bishop's family.' She recalled a time when her children were ill and there were builders working in the house and how she had 'just wished so desperately for someone to come and put their arms round me . . . for somebody to say POOR YOU.' Another spoke about the time the doctor came to see her husband. They had not been in the diocese very long and still felt rather friendless. The doctor turned to her and said 'And how are YOU?' at which she burst into tears.

This emphasizes how necessary it is to nurture the friendships we already have and to establish some new ones if possible. In some cases, parents or other members of the family might be expected to be supportive and understanding but this varies considerably. One wife told me that her own family, although clergy themselves, were given to remarks such as, 'Is P out in the diocese again tonight then . . . being very important?', appearing not to realize how hurtful this could be or how vulnerable the family felt already. Yet, in contrast to this, another couple make a point of sending a copy of their weekly diary to their parents, knowing that it will be prayed over each day. Many of us find that adult children can be very caring, but for each story illustrating this attitude there appears to be another one which shows the opposite. Our eldest son admitted that it took him some time to realize that we might have our own problems. After being known as 'The Altar Boy' in the rugby club, he took care not to tell his future wife about us for a few weeks after he first met her!

Parochial clergy are ambivalent in their attitudes. A bishop's son suggested to me that bishops are seen as winners, especially if they have been parish priests themselves. So, while in some ways their past experience helps because it is acknowledged that they understand, have stood in the same shoes, there can also be a vague resentment, summed up by 'lucky for some!' It would be misleading to suggest that these experiences are common to all bishops' families but there is no doubt that many suffer in silence. Others, particularly wives, find the privacy most welcome and are glad to do their own thing.

New bishops: the wider church

In the past, it has simply been taken for granted that bishops and their wives needed no training as such, with the result that many have found themselves 'swimming through glue for at least a year', as it was graphically described to me. More recently, some thought has been given to this problem and an Archbishop's Advisor for Bishops' Ministry has been appointed. One of his briefs is to set up consultations for new bishops to reflect together on the experience of their first months in office. Wives are invited for the final weekend, giving an opportunity to share some of the fears and perhaps the shocks of the new situation, even the fact that the husband is now officially referred to as 'My Lord' while the wife remains plain Mrs!

This 'English situation' caused great amusement at the Lambeth Conference, when about 400 wives accompanied their husbands to Canterbury for three weeks in 1988. We held our own conference beside theirs, with a separate programme. It was one of the greatest privileges I have had as a bishop's wife to be a member of that gathering, from all over the Anglican Communion. We began each day with Bible study in groups. I was the only wife, out of fifteen in my group, from an English diocese. There were six from Africa (only one white), four from America, and one each from New Zealand, Canada, Bermuda and Scotland. It was an education in itself: an unforgettable oasis of international sharing between bishops and their wives, whose common heritage, however, diverse their backgrounds and situations, was their commitment to the Christian Way. Bishops' wives in America and Australia have produced their own books, called respectively *Side by Side* and *Partners in Purple*, followed by a recent one in this country, each with the purpose of helping new bishops' wives. All reveal how different we are as individuals, yet how similar our experiences are in so many ways. They might almost be called handbooks for survival, showing that others share our situation too.

Personal reflections

'A thick skin, a loving heart and one blind eye.' These were the words which Michael used to express what he felt were the qualities he would need as a bishop. His consecration, on St Paul's day in York Minster in 1976, was the beginning of a new way of life for our whole family. I had many personal tussles in accepting it, both beforehand and for some time afterwards. One day I was reading my Bible when a familiar passage struck me with force. It was the story of the healing of the blind man in St John's Gospel (chapter 9). He was not healed only by Jesus' action, daubing earth mixed with spittle on his eyes, but also by going and washing in the Pool of Siloam. To have his eyes opened HE had to take action too.

It took me some time to see that in fact God was taking the first step in curing MY blindness. After that it was up to me. The blind man had not asked to be made to see and neither had I. There was also a pool of Siloam for me — the acceptance of my new situation and finding out how best to use my newly acquired sight. Without my parochial shell, my busy house, my long-founded, deep relationships, I had to ask myself once again who I was. It can be a very disturbing experience in your forties! Now, many years later, I am so glad that God uprooted me and made me aware that perhaps I had almost ceased to grow. I was given a new vision and limitless opportunities not only to understand other people's situations but also for my own personal growth. If all this sounds too smug, perhaps I should admit that while the blind man only had to bathe once to see clearly, I still find myself returning to my own Pool of Siloam from time to time.

Not Always
Murder at the Vicarage·

ANN E. HENSHALL

I loved living in a vicarage — most of the time! Having married a fellow-student five weeks before he was ordained, the reality of parish life was both better and worse than I had expected — but never dull.

It was only when my husband ceased to be a parish priest and I left vicarage life after nearly twenty years that I really began to comprehend what I had lost. In physical terms my 'bereavement' meant no church and parish hall just across the lawn. In terms of a community I now found myself belonging to such a wide geographical area (a diocese) that I did not quite know where I fitted in.

I love meeting people, but there is great value in having one particular group to which we 'belong' without too much conscious effort. Spiritually I missed the regular services (formerly on the doorstep) in which we took part as a family. Since my husband no longer belonged to one particular parish, my children and I had to make the effort to go to church — usually without father.

We hear a good deal nowadays about the problems and difficulties of being a clergy wife —

· Reprinted from the *Church Times*, 27 February 1987

the negative side. It sometimes makes me rather sad because I have always felt that there were so many positives, so many advantages, while in no way denying the disadvantages.

Rose-coloured?

It may be thought that after eleven years I am looking back on vicarage life with rose-coloured spectacles, but I honestly do not think that this is the case. I am in almost daily contact with clergy wives, varied as they are in character and attitude. It does seem to be true, perhaps inevitable, that the ones we hear most about are the unhappy or the actively hostile ones. I certainly know many who are very happy and plenty who enjoy their role.

I use the term 'role' advisedly. There are some clergy wives who decry the word altogether. I remember being taken to task on one occasion by two vehement wives who declared that they were not clergy wives but 'themselves'. I know what they meant very well but I pointed out then (and I have yet to be convinced that it is not true) that the calling of our husbands affects our public and private image in a way that happens to no other profession.

My father was a barrister. I can never remember my mother being introduced as 'the barrister's wife'. My father's clients came to his chambers, not to our home. Incoming telephone calls were almost entirely concerned with private and family matters. The doorbell went infrequently.

Neither phone nor doorbell went at mealtimes.

As a family we were not involved in my father's work, rarely saw him in court and did not know his clients. However we did complain at times that most of his friends talked 'shop'!

There is no doubt that the vicarage is not a private house in some senses, though with care it can definitely be a real home. Nobody today wants it to be different or unapproachable. On the other hand there are always some parishioners who will take unfair advantage, and it is often difficult to know how to deal tactfully with such situations.

Whether a vicar's wife is deeply involved in the life of the parish or has a full- or part-time job outside the home, as sixty per cent of all women have nowadays (which incidentally does not preclude her involvement anyway), there is no denying the fact that the doorbell and telephone will ring in her home very frequently, often at most inconvenient times. Parishioners vary in their understanding of her needs, but most expect her to have patience and care in dealing with theirs.

Some theological colleges take care in helping to prepare ordinands' wives for parish life, since over half our ordinands in training nowadays are married. Perhaps this should be a priority.

There are three basic paths to becoming a clergy wife. The first is my own, which consists of marrying before or shortly after ordination a man whose vocation is already recognized and accepted. The second — more usual in the past, when students were discouraged from marrying — involves that of meeting a curate or vicar already working in a parish whose calling and way of life is clear to him, to his intended wife and everybody else.

The third path involves the wife who married a layman, perhaps a shopkeeper, a dentist or a teacher, who feels at some later date that he has a vocation to the ministry. It is sometimes for her a much more difficult transition. After all, the others should have had a pretty good idea of what they expected ! The wife of a late ordinand told me that if she had not shared in her husband's certainty about his vocation, she did not believe that he should have gone ahead, as she regarded his first vocation as his marriage to her.

The practical advantages of living in a vicarage can easily be taken for granted as they become familiar. The clergy may not be overpaid in financial terms, but there is inbuilt job-security going hand in hand with a (usually) pleasant house, maintained at a reasonable-to-good standard without expense to the family who live in it, whereas many laymen live with a mortgage hanging over their heads and may have to forego their holidays because the roof is leaking or the drive needs repairing. These particular worries are not shared by the clergy-house.

I have personally been a visitor in well over half the vicarages in my diocese. Many families admit that they might well not have such substantial homes if they were in secular employment.

The variety of houses, although they tend to be increasingly modern and easy-to-run, gives the clergy family plenty of choice, so that a family of five or six can usually find as suitable accommodation as can the family of three. The same applies to the parish, the church and the type of ministry, for within reason a priest can choose in which part of the country he wishes to work and what kind of parish — whether city, suburb, town or country — best suits his ministry.

This contrasts greatly with many other 'jobs' where there is little likelihood of change, promotion or even choice of location.

Parish life offers great variety and the opportunity to experiment, meet new people, work with different groups and have friends and acquaintances from every kind of background. The possibility of moving is always there and the freehold means that a clergy family can move, within reason, when it suits them, with consideration for the age and education of their children.

When a clergy family does move, however hard they may find it and however deep their roots may be, they very quickly become part of the next parish community — generally well motivated and welcoming towards them. This very fact may perhaps blind the clergyman and his wife to the more painful experience of most lay families, who have to build a new life from scratch and make a network of relationships in order to become part of their new communities — if they can find such a thing apart from the church.

Babysitters

Not only do the clergy wife and her family thus have an opportunity to live in the area of her choice, from inner city to rural countryside, but during the years of her husband's ministry she may move with ease from one to the other. My own experience included a seaside parish, a Lancashire mill town and a market town which changed its character fairly rapidly to something more akin to a sophisticated city dormitory. All were quite different and we found that living in such varied communities had a very broadening effect. The disadvantage of having no natural roots is far outweighed, in my opinion, by the valuable lessons thus offered.

The vicar's wife has also, if she wants it, a built-in system of babysitters, support and help in times of illness and a husband who, however busy, is usually able in times of family crisis to make himself available because his work is based on home. Clergymen who do not have a day off, the kind who boast of being 'workaholics', are very unfair to their wives and families (and to their parishes).

Many clergy families find time to spend together. I believe that all could if they chose. A parish day is relatively flexible compared with that of many laymen whose hours are fixed, even if their evenings are free, so that clergy children are sometimes the lucky ones whose fathers can get to school events on weekdays.

'For better, for worse but not for lunch!', I used to cry occasionally when I was having to get yet another meal. Yet I know that wives whose husbands are home at lunch-time tend to lead much more contented lives. They can make that break in the day special, even if it is interrupted. Their conversation will most likely be centred on the parish, but at least the wife knows the people who are mentioned and can share in the hopes and fears and give informed advice (if asked!).

I know a vicar's daughter, now married to an accountant, who says what a vast difference she finds after growing up in a clergy household. There is really no way that she can get to know her husband's clients or share in his work. Her children are still young and she says how little they see of their father, who often returns home after they have gone to bed.

Mealtimes are very important to family life. With a little planning most clergy families really should be able to eat regularly together.

The relative lack of privacy may have its disadvantages, but loneliness — or at any rate physical loneliness — is almost impossible to experience in a vicarage. This may mean that clergy families may be unable to appreciate just how terrible loneliness can be, or how prevalent it is in the modern world.

As for the problems of clergy children, I believe that these can be greatly exaggerated - not the problems themselves, but the fact that they are the problems of 'clergy' children. There are some particular ones, naturally, but they should not be got out of proportion. Most children have problems, whatever their parents do for a living. Most teenagers find their parents 'square' and lacking in understanding and most parents find their teenagers selfish and unco-operative.

Vicarage children have a marvellous advantage over most of their peers, in that they have (usually) a more stable family life. They may resent their parents' involvement with parishioners and commitment beyond the immediate home, but they learn that life is more than narrow acquisition and ambition. If they are lucky they remain reasonably immune from the world of callous competition and status symbols.

Until recently, clergy couples used to find the prospect of retirement rather daunting. However, the acceptance of the measure requiring retirement from a beneficed office by the age of seventy and the helpful attitude of the Pensions Board have greatly improved the situation. There is no doubt that the provision for widows when clergymen die in office is not easy, nor is that of wives whose marriages break down, since they have to leave their homes in addition to all the other difficulties. However, it is doubtful whether the widows or alienated wives of laymen really fare very much better, and they probably do not receive as much love and sympathy in their grief.

I am not wishing to ignore the question of marriage breakdown in clergy families. While realizing that some cases may be due to particular tensions and conditions of parish life, I think it is largely unfair to blame the job for difficulties in marriage. There is so much more opportunity for a shared life than in most marriages. I believe that the relationship within the marriage itself is the most important thing.

When the husband is a doctor or a bus driver, the different periods of married life are subject to tension and strain, due to work or lack of it, the number of children or lack of them, the possible conflict of interests, hours of work and state of health. When these apply to a clergy household, it is often blamed on the job!

160

In actual fact, if bridges have been built in the parish, real relationships established and mutual support exists, these problems should be able to be resolved better in that job than anywhere else. A clergy wife is first and foremost just that — a wife. She may or may not do the flowers or lead the ladies' organizations but she really does need to share an understanding of her husband's vocation. In the Church of England we do not ask our clergy wives to be fellow-officers with their husbands, as is required by the Salvation Army.

Common aim

While in no way ignoring the difficulties, the disappointments and the great variety of experience and response, and while aware of the different gifts and characters of those who minister, I can think of no other work in which the potential for 'job satisfaction' is so great. Non-Christians may be indifferent or hostile, congregations may be gossipy or awkward, but so much emanates from the priest himself and from his household.

After all, we were never told that life would be easy! The priest and his wife have a wonderful opportunity to create together a Christian community and not just a 'religious congregation'.

They live at the hub of the wheel: they know some of the anxieties, the hurts, the fears and failures of so many parishioners. If they are prepared to share them, they find great mutual comfort and love in belonging to that extended family of the church.

In the past, communities were smaller and more

interdependent. Modern transport, cities and the media have changed all that. In today's world the parish community with a common purpose is the nearest thing most of us will ever have to the old world where everybody knew everybody else. We are very lucky if we belong to such a group.

For my part, I know that for every kindness I gave I was repaid a hundred-fold. I already had a sense of humour and I tried to develop a thicker skin! I found great joy in belonging to a community which, while most definitely only 'saints in the making' really shared the basic common ideals of the Christian life.

The last words must be those of my daughter. She was eleven when we left the vicarage. Recently she stayed for ten weeks with a vicarage family. She loved it. She looked back on our own experience, remembered the fun and the sense of belonging to a big 'family'. 'I suppose we weren't very private', she said. 'You know, I didn't realize it until now, but really we were very spoiled!'

Appendix 2

Parsons at Risk[*]

'Friendly vicar runs off with blonde verger' is the sort of story that some of our more sensational newspapers leap upon with great joy . . . for every one case that hits the headlines, there are possibly half a dozen which are hushed up. . . . A practical and helpful course would be to look at the reasons . . . then to suggest what can be done about them.

It is obvious that the clergy face a particular occupational hazard. Most work long hours . . . are out most evenings of the week as well as in the daytime. It is the wife who suffers most, especially if she has a young family and is tied to the home. On top of this she is expected to act as a deputy door and telephone answerer . . . caterer when her husband invites guests to a meal . . . inn-keeper when they stay overnight. She acts as welfare officer to the tramps who arrive on the vicarage doorstep. Some wives find it all a bit too much. They see little of their husbands and grow resentful that they are left to cope with his work. . . .

Two practical suggestions are . . . Clergy wives should be told what they are in for before they marry a prospective parson . . . clergy should not take their wives and families so much for granted. . . .

_____

[*] Excerpts from an article by Michael Smout in the *Church Times*, 23 November 1973, discussing why clergymen fall victim more easily to matrimonial and other problems.

Unfortunately it is possible for the clergy to make themselves into martyrs and to find a peculiar satisfaction in overwork ... the consequence sometimes is that he is drawn apart from his wife. He is then peculiarly open to a relationship with another woman ... It can start off innocently enough as a pastoral concern for someone in the congregation ... The tragic thing is that the clergy are not warned as to the vulnerable position they are in.

How is this sort of situation to be avoided? More pastoral care for the clergy would certainly help the problem. ... The bishop is pastor pastorum, in theory at least. Unfortunately he has so many other tasks that make demands upon his time that his calling of caring for his clergy gets squeezed out. This is tragic and thought must be given to a solution to this particular problem.

Obviously [the clergyman's] closest confidant should be his wife. But how many find it easy to share with their wives? He comes in at night having talked all through the day and only wants to flop down in a chair and watch TV. His wife wants to talk her share but gets no response. ... Pity the clergyman who confines his friendships to his fellow clergy, showing that he is probably too proud to allow members of his congregation to minister to him rather than vice versa.

The clergy are expected to be experts at dealing with other people's problems but how much effort is being made to deal with the problems of the clergy themselves? The God-given ministry of every man could be revitalized by adequate pastoral care before it is too late.

Clergy's Matrimonial Problems·

Sir,
Much of Michael Smout's article on 'Parsons at Risk' (*Church Times* 23 November) was sound common sense. I should, however, like to question his main point that they are 'more than usually prone to matrimonial and other problems'.

Many laymen I know have equally difficult situations to deal with. They have long business hours coupled with the tedium of commuting home to wives frustrated by boredom and loneliness, in addition to noisy toddlers or difficult teenagers. They are often away from home for long periods, sometimes accompanied by attractive secretaries.

The 'workaholic' may be a priest or a layman and may well be so tied up in his work specifically to avoid the problems of home.

As a young wife who had married a fellow-student I was sometimes saddened at the slightly bitter or frustrated attitudes of some older clergy wives. Seventeen years later I am more able to appreciate how easily this can come about.

All the same, the clergy wife does not have the anxieties of high mortgages and job security which may worry her lay sister. She may wish that she had said 'For better, for worse, but not for

* Letter to the *Church Times*, 7 December 1973

165

lunch!' but even so she must realize that seeing her husband during the day has more advantages than disadvantages. She might well like the long holidays suggested by Michael Smout, but she must know that few lay families can afford them either.

It would seem that the breakdown of a clergy marriage is no different from that of a lay marriage. The key to the success of a lay marriage lies in the two people themselves and in their attitude to the marriage. The clergy wife who becomes depressed in middle age might well exhibit the same symptoms if she were a dentist's wife. The priest who loses heart might well be equally downcast if he were an oil-distributor.

Other people's marriages are easy to view from the outside. The clergy and their wives are constantly called upon to give advice and succour. Perhaps they simply expect their own marriages to stand firm indefinitely without the need for reappraisal or therapy.

The relationship between husband and wife, clerical or otherwise, has to be a conscious thing, recognizing that time does not stand still. Men need to be shown affection in the same way as children — a fact which many women fail to recognize.

Living right at the hub of the Christian community can 'petrify' some people's ideas. If these include their attitudes towards their own marriages, then they may wake up one morning and wonder what happened to the relationship they took for granted.

In no other sphere can a wife share so much in

her husband's work if she so wishes. If she does not share in this interest, then perhaps her husband would be happier outside the confines of a parish, where his household would not be directly involved in his work.

There is a positive side to the life of the clergy family which the article perhaps failed to stress. Bishop Hensley Henson said many years ago: 'It is impossible to overestimate the spiritual value of a genuine Christian family life in the vicarage.' Surely this applies equally today, and perhaps clergy families should grumble less and try to realize afresh the joy with which most of us must have started out on our marriages.

Ann Henshall
The Vicarage,
Townfield Road,
Altrincham, Cheshire.

Suggestions
for Further Reading

Michael Ramsey, *The Christian Priest Today.* (SPCK, 1972, 1986).

Antony Russell, *The Clerical Profession.* (SPCK, 1980).

Michael Henshall, *Dear Nicholas: A father's letter to his newly ordained son* (Churchman Publishing, 1989).

Faith in the City. The Report of the Archbishop of Canterbury's Commission on Urban Priority Areas. (Church House Publishing, 1985).

Faith in the Countryside. The Report of the Archbishops' Commission on Rural Areas. (Churchman Publishing Ltd, 1990).

Peter Rutter, *Sex in the Forbidden Zone.* (Unwin Paperbacks, 1990).

Wanda Nash, *Living with God in the Vicarage.* Pastoral Series No 42, (Grove Booklets, 1990).

Couples in Ministry Ministry Committee of the Diocese of Sheffield (1988). (Obtainable from M. Selby, 25, Bannham Road, Darnall, Sheffield S9 4PG).

Additional literature can also be obtained from:

The Advisory Board of Ministry
(ABM, formerly ACCM),
Church House,
Great Smith Street,
London SW1P 3NZ.

The Church of England Pensions Board,
7 Little College Street,
London SW1P 3SF.

Also published by

TRIANGLE

GROWN MEN DO CRY
Stories of a Vicar's life
by Roy Catchpole

Stories of everyday life in a Nottinghamshire parish from the only ex-convict clergyman in the Church of England.

SEVEN FOR A SECRET THAT'S NEVER BEEN TOLD
Healing the wounds of sexual abuse in childhood
by Tracy Hansen

A moving account of a survivor of child sexual abuse working through the trauma induced by the return of repressed memories.

THE GAP
Christians and people who don't go to church
by Jack Burton

Bus driver and Methodist minister Jack Burton describes his unique vocation of bridging the gap between two cultures.

FROM NUN TO MUM
An ex-nun adopts twins from South America
by Clare Richards

A personal account of one Christian's journey in faith with a serious message for the church.

LIFE LATER ON
Older people and the Church
by Ann Webber

Brings us closer to the experience and insights of older people, describing how they can make up a vital part of most Christian activities.

TRi∧NGle

Books
can be obtained from
all good bookshops.
In case of difficulty,
or for a complete list of our books,
contact:
SPCK Mail Order
36 Steep Hill
Lincoln
LN2 1LU
(tel: 0522 527 486)